CONTENTS

DEDICATION

This book is dedicated to my late Father, Owen Edwards, who just a few weeks before he passed away was proof reading sections of this work. He was a professional railwayman and loved the Isle of Man. Thanks Dad, I trust you would have approved.

All photographs not otherwise credited where taken by the author.

Produced and Designed by Lily Publications Ltd

Printed and bound by Gomer Press Ltd., Wales

© Lily Publications 2010

INTRODUCTION

It is some 17 years since my first book on the railways of the Isle of Man was published and what an eventful 17 years it has been.

Pretty much the entire length of both the Steam Railway and the Manx Electric have been relaid, with new rail and sleepers, the Steam Railway has two new carriage sheds, the Manx Electric a new top shed at Derby Castle and the recently completed replacement shed at Laxey. The Snaefell shed has also been replaced with a modern structure providing much needed maintenance facilities. There have been three different Directors but thankfully what has not changed, is the atmosphere and the vintage rolling stock.

Elsewhere the continued restoration at Groudle has produced an overall roof at Lhen Coan, a new locomotive shed, replacement of the Sea Lion Rocks building, a replica battery electric locomotive and for this season a new shop. The Orchid Line has had two extensions, a new carriage shed, several new buildings and has carried its 100,000th passenger. The Laxey Mines Railway has been revived complete with two super replica locomotives, while a new private line has been built in the grounds of the Crogga estate. The Manx Electric celebrated its centenary in 1993,

Snaefell in 1995, Groudle in 1996, the Steam completed 125 years service in 1998. The centenary of the completion of the Manx Electric through to Ramsey came in 1999 and the Horse Tramway completed its 125th season in 2001.

A book of this nature leads the Author to seek assistance from many people and my sincere thanks go to each and every person who has assisted with this publication. Special thanks, as always, go to the Management and staff of Isle of Man Transport, The Douglas Horse Tramway, Groudle Glen Railway, Laxey Mines Railway, The Orchid Line and Chris Beauman and his staff at Crogga. Richard Davis, Jack Dibnah, John Messenger and Tony Wilson have assisted with information and photographs. Thanks are due to Miles and Linda Cowsill at Lily Publications, my late Father for checking the main text sections of this book and my wife Irene for her support throughout this project.

Whatever your preference, be it steam, electric or even horse traction, sit back and enjoy this journey with the Trains and Trams of the Isle of Man.

Barry Edwards
Ballasalla, Isle of Man
January 2010

With the summit of Snaefell as a backdrop, car No 2 makes its descent with a full load of passengers. The gulley up the hillside just behind the tram is home to one of several tributaries of the Laxey River.

Douglas Railway Station - June 2009. (Miles Cowsill)

CHAPTER ONE

THE STEAM RAILWAY

The first attempts to build a railway from Douglas to Peel were made in 1860 and 1863 but neither project came to anything, nor did a scheme registered with Tynwald in 1865. Eventually, in April 1870, a meeting was called in Douglas, to which all interested parties were invited, to come up with a plan that would not suffer the fate of previous attempts.

Agreement was reached in principle to form a railway company to build a line linking Douglas with Peel, Ramsey and Castletown, with a projected extension to Port Erin that was intending to have a steamer service to Holyhead in North Wales.

The Isle of Man Railway Company was registered in December 1870 with a capital of £200,000 but, following a survey of the routes, it was realised that this was not sufficient. Approaches were made overseas and, after a short while, the company was joined by The Duke of Sutherland and Mr John Pender. The Duke became Chairman for the first seven years, being followed by Mr Pender.

In 1872 tenders were invited to construct a 3'0" gauge railway from Douglas to Peel and Port Erin. Four replies were received and the contract was awarded to Messrs Watson & Smith of London.

Three locomotives were ordered from Beyer, Peacock of Gorton Foundry, Manchester in 1872. They were 2-4-0T locomotives with copper-capped chimneys, brass domes and brass numerals on the chimneys. Eventually 15 such locomotives were delivered to the railway, a decision that proved useful in later years as it was possible to interchange most parts between locomotives. The livery was to be green with a black smokebox.

No.1 Sutherland arrived in March 1873 and Nos.2 and 3, Derby and Pender, in June. Rolling stock was delivered from the Metropolitan Carriage & Wagon Co. of Saltley, consisting of 29 four-wheeled coaches including two guards vans. Various items of freight stock also arrived.

The first train ran on the 1st May 1873 with the Duke of Sutherland on the footplate of No.1, the train formed of open wagons with seating fitted. No.1 came off the rails at Peel, the construction contractor's locomotive being summoned to return the train to Douglas. The Duke returned to the railway on the 1st July 1873 to take his seat in the directors' saloon forming part of the 12-coach official opening train. Locomotive No.1 hauled the train carrying suitable decoration and a banner reading 'Douglas and Peel United'. Huge crowds turned out to welcome the railway to the Island and to watch the train clatter past at speeds of up to 25 mph, faster than any Islander had seen before.

Meanwhile, over 400 men were busy pushing on with the Port Erin line which was proving a more difficult task with its steep gradients and sharper curves. In June 1874 the contractor pulled out, leaving the railway company to complete the line, which in the end cost £9,875 per mile to build. This meant that economies were made on stations with only simple wooden structures being provided. The line opened without ceremony on the 1st August 1874.

Two further locomotives, Nos.4 and 5, Loch and Mona were delivered in 1874 to work the new line and the rolling stock fleet was increased to 56 coaches, still all four-wheeled. Locomotives Nos.6 and 7, Peveril and Tynwald, were delivered in 1875 and 1880 respectively.

The residents in the north of the Island thought they would be next to get a railway but, despite its initial intentions, the company announced that it had no plans for such an extension. The northerners decided to go it alone and the Manx Northern Railway Company was formed in 1877, and given government consent in 1878 to build a 16-mile line from St Johns to Ramsey.

The contract to build the line, that included several viaducts, was awarded to J. & W. Grainger of Glasgow, with completion due by the 1st July 1879. Two locomotives were ordered from Sharp, Stewart & Company of Manchester, No.1 Ramsey and No.2 Northern. Coaches were all from Swansea Wagon Company and on Cleminson patent six-wheel chassis. A third locomotive, No.3 Thornhill was ordered for delivery in 1880, this time from Beyer, Peacock and similar to those being supplied to the Isle of Man Railway Company.

Two and a half miles south of St Johns, the small mining village of Foxdale was producing 4,000 tons of ore annually

Although the first train of the day does not leave Port Erin until 10.20, the fireman sign on around three hours earlier to begin the preparation of the locomotive for the day's work. Here with the shed clock showing just about 07.45, Rodney Swift cleans out the tubes of No.13 Kissack in Port Erin shed.

Having cleaned out the tubes, the next job is to light the fire. A few old sleepers and some rags soaked in paraffin are laid out in the bottom of the firebox. A further soaked rag is placed on the shovel and lit, then placed in the firebox. Soon a good fire is beginning to heat the water in the tanks.

The next job is to polish all the brasswork on the locomotive. Starting on the footplate, Rodney gives the firebox surround a good polish after applying plenty of Brasso

After many years storage in the old Douglas carriage shed, No.6 Peveril was cosmetically restored by the Isle of Man Steam Railway Supporters' Association. It now stands on display in the Railway Museum at Port Erin. The coach behind the locomotive is F36.

Alongside No.6 in the Museum is No.16 Mannin, the last new locomotive built for the Isle of Man Railway Company in 1926. On the wall to the right of the locomotive is a collection of headboards used for recent events.

Pairs coach F75 is also preserved in the Museum. On a chassis dating from 1926 it has the bodies of four-wheeled coaches A12 and C9.

No.13 Kissack emerges from the locomotive shed at Port Erin to take on water and make the final preparations for the first departure of the day. The heap of ash will be left from the night before when the fire was dropped after arrival with the last train from Douglas.

Diesel locomotive No.17 Viking captured shortly after arrival at Port Erin with a lengthy train from Douglas. One of the steam locomotives is on the other end of the train.

To mark the 40th anniversary of the 'Ailsa' period in 2007, No.10 G. H. Wood was repainted into Ailsa green livery. Seen here awaiting departure from Port Erin with the first commuter train of the 2007 Centenary TT Festival, the 07.45 departure allowed well-lit platform side pictures, not normally possible. The large shadows are created by the buses parked adjacent to the platform.

and the idea of a railway linking Foxdale with the other lines at St Johns was actively considered. The Foxdale Railway Company was formed in 1882, managing to lease itself to the Manx Northern Railway for 50 years, even before construction started.

The stations at Foxdale and St Johns were constructed by Hugh Kennedy & Sons of Glasgow. No expense was spared and by June 1886 the line was in full swing, carrying tons of ore each day. A fourth locomotive was delivered, this time an 0-6-0T from Dubs & Co., Scotland, No.4 Caledonia.

The final years of the l800s saw the Isle of Man Railway go from strength to strength, 26 bogie coaches being delivered by 1896 and locomotives No.8 Fenella and No.9 Douglas arriving in 1894 and 1896. Douglas station was rebuilt with the impressive forecourt that still exists today, the carriage shed was built and extensions were added to the locomotive sheds and workshops.

Port Erin, Port St. Mary, Peel and Castletown stations were also rebuilt, as was that at Port Soderick where a passing loop was added. The tourist boom had not gone unnoticed by other railway promoters and the opening of the Derby Castle to Groudle electric railway, which

eventually reached Ramsey in 1899, provided some interesting competition. The Isle of Man Railway Company advertised a 68-minute journey from Douglas to Ramsey, while the electric railway offered 70 minutes.

The Foxdale Railway went into voluntary liquidation in 1891, leaving the Manx Northern to carry out the requirements of the remaining lease, until in 1904 the Manx Northern was itself in trouble. The Isle of Man Railway was approached and an Act of Tynwald allowed the purchase of the Manx Northern for £60,000 and the Foxdale Railway for £7,000.

New coaches were ordered and the four Manx Northern Railway locomotives were taken into Isle of Man Railway stock. Two more locomotives arrived from Beyer, Peacock in 1905, No.10 G.H. Wood and No.11 Maitland.

Two further locomotives arrived from Beyer, Peacock in 1908 and 1910, No.12 Hutchinson and No.13 Kissack. Peel station building was rebuilt in 1908, Port Erin was enlarged in 1911, and the canopies were added at Douglas. One million passengers were carried for the first time in 1913. The Foxdale mines closed in 1914 but the passenger service continued, usually with just one coach.

In anticipation of good patronage, sadly not fulfilled, the train was presented to intending passengers with all its doors open. A lonely Jackdaw seems to be the only taker!

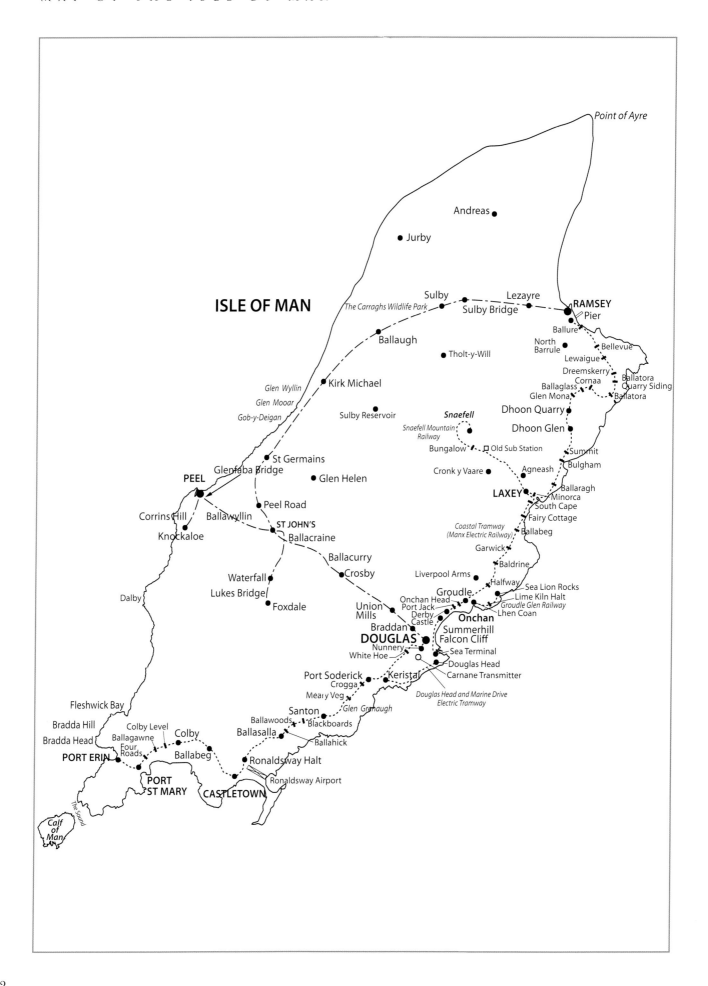

ISLE OF MAN

The very first train of the 2008 season awaits departure from Port Erin, on the 17th March, with No.12 Hutchinson in charge. During the early and late season, trains are usually only three coaches but, the first and last days often attract good passenger loads and justify the fourth coach.

The outbreak of war in 1914 reduced the number of visitors to the Island but, from 1915, the railway was called upon to operate trains between Peel and Knockaloe over a specially constructed line serving a camp for 20,000 prisoners of war. The former Manx Northern locomotive, the Caledonia, worked the line as it was the best to cope with the steep gradients.

Visitors returned to the Island by the thousand after the war and, despite the rising costs of materials and wages, and the introduction of the eight-hour working day, the railway continued to flourish. Much overtime was worked by the staff to keep the frequent service operating and, during the winters, all attention was turned to maintenance of locomotives, rolling stock and track.

No.16 Mannin was delivered in 1926 and was the last locomotive ordered new by the railway and the last completely new coach, F49 also arrived. Manxland Bus Services were granted permission to operate motor bus services on a range of routes from Douglas. The railway response was to cut fares, reduce journey times and increase the number of timetabled trains, particularly during the evening.

The early bus years culminated in the formation of Isle of Man Road Services Ltd in 1930, resulting in co-operation between the bus and rail operators, 'Freedom of the Island' tickets being offered jointly. The latter years of the 1930s saw an annual rail passenger level of around 750,000.

World War II brought more work for the railway but, as the Knockaloe camp had been demolished, hotels were commandeered to house prisoners of war. Training camps at Jurby and Castletown took passenger numbers above those of peacetime and school journeys came back from the buses because of shortages of tyres and fuel. Over 14,000 special trains had operated by the end of hostilities in 1945.

Visitors once again returned in large numbers in 1946. However, the steam locomotives were all in need of overhaul, several requiring complete new boilers, of which three were ordered and fitted. During 1945, No. 7 had been cannibalised for much needed spares and No.2 went the same way in 1951. Nos.3, 4 and 9 were also withdrawn from service, in need of new boilers.

The post-war boom ended in 1956 with over a million passengers carried for the last time, the numbers steadily declining thereafter as air travel took holidaymakers off to other parts of the world. Costs continued to rise, receipts fell and service cuts started. Sunday services were withdrawn

Shortly after 10.00 on Monday the 17th March 2008, No.12 Hutchinson eases down the platform at Port Erin to couple to her train and prepare for departure to Douglas with the first train of the season.

While a petrol locomotive is used to get the passenger coaches from the carriage shed in the morning, the operating steam locomotive usually puts them away again at the end of the working day. Here we see No.11 Maitland gently pushing a rake of coaches into the shed for overnight storage.

Port Erin was treated to a carriage shed in 1998 allowing overnight undercover storage of the precious rolling stock. Inside the shed on the 12th October 2008 were F26 with F25, F63, F62 and F21 behind and F10 on the adjacent track.

One of the railway Simplex locomotives hides away in the depths of Port Erin carriage shed during October 2008. This locomotive is often used to shunt the passenger stock into the platform at the beginning of each day.

The route of the steam railway lends itself to photography throughout its length, there being a number of superb vantage points to choose from. Here we see No.10 G. H. Wood shortly after leaving Port Erin and passing the Ballamaddrell estate. The recently built houses of Erin Way are visible on the left of the picture.

The first station stop on the journey to Douglas is Port St. Mary. Negotiating the points into the siding, No.12 Hutchinson arrives with the first train of the day, no doubt on time at 10.22.

Port St. Mary has just a single platform with no passing facility. Here we see No.10 G. H. Wood hiding behind her own steam whilst working a Port Erin bound train on the penultimate day of service for 2008.

altogether and winter services were reduced to school traffic level without much loss of receipts.

No.11 Maitland received a badly needed new boiler in 1959 but replacements for Nos.1, 6, 13 and 16 were considered unnecessary. Service cuts continued and winter services became virtually non-existent.

Two former County Donegal diesel railcars were obtained in 1961, at £160 each, and were refurbished in time to work the Peel service that winter. The situation on the railway was now serious and the outlook bleak.

On the 7th July 1963 Her Majesty Queen Elizabeth the Queen Mother arrived on the Island and travelled on the railway from Douglas to Kirk Braddan in coach F36, No.11 Maitland doing the honours at the front.

A loss of £8,000 was made in 1965 and all winter services were cancelled in order to carry out much needed maintenance; this too was later cancelled without warning. No trains ran in 1966 but a report into the future of the line recognised the importance of the railway to the community. The Isle of Man Railway Supporters' Association was formed, offering to assist in any way it could. Relief arrived from the Marquis of Ailsa, who agreed to lease the line for 21 years with an opt-out clause after five years.

Hundreds of people turned out on the 3rd June 1967, the occasion of the railway's reopening. Five special trains ran to Peel, with services to Ramsey and Castletown as well and a frequent daytime service operated throughout the railway for the rest of that season.

No.4 Loch received a new boiler in 1968, returning to service on the last day of that season. However, mounting losses again caused the season to be cut short, the last train from Ramsey running on the 6th September and the last from Peel the next day. The Peel and Ramsey lines never reopened.

The Tourist Board agreed in 1968 to assist in keeping the Port Erin line open for three years. No.13 received a new boiler and passenger numbers increased slightly but the Marquis was still losing money and announced that he would take the five-year option. It is estimated that he lost around £43,000 during his stay but, without him, the railway would almost certainly have closed and been lost forever.

In 1971 the Tourist Board offered the railway company further support for another three years and costs were reduced by only operating a Monday to Friday service. Her

When driving around the Island it always pays to have the camera in the car. On this occasion this policy proved its worth, when I was caught by the gates at Port St. Mary and took full advantage of the bright sunny day. No.4 Loch departs with the early afternoon train to Douglas.

The sight and sound of a narrow gauge steam train making its way through the Manx countryside is something to be savoured. Heading towards Douglas, an unidentified locomotive leads three coaches approaching Four Roads level crossing with the houses of Ballagawne Road in the background.

On Monday the 29th May 2007, No.10 G. H. Wood storms past Ballagawne Crossing with the 07.45 commuter service to Douglas. The building partly obscured by the train is the former crossing keeper's cottage. The driver peers out to check that all is well ahead.

Unlike the rest of the fleet, No.4 Loch carries its number and a three legs of Mann on its front buffer beam. Approaching Ballagawne Crossing with a heavy Port Erin bound service, the operating season sufficiently well advanced that the passing of the train is ignored by the sheep in the neighbouring field.

On this occasion there was not time to get out of the car, so the picture of No.13 Kissack passing Four Roads crossing was captured from the driving seat. No doubt the passengers on the train will be waving to the car drivers in the hope of a response.

The station at Colby Level crossing, known as The Level must boast one of the shortest platforms on any UK railway. It is one of four request stops on the line, passengers intending to alight must inform the guard, those wishing to join the train should give a clear hand signal to the driver, who will make his approach heard by using the whistle.

Colby is the next stop on our journey to Douglas. No.12 Hutchinson awaits the right of way to proceed. Unusually the trains use what would normally be considered as the down loop here, the up loop seeing little use. The station building, originally from Braddan, is just visible to the left of the picture.

Majesty The Queen travelled on the line from Castletown to Douglas on the 2nd August 1972, the total number of passengers carried that year being the best for some time.

On the 1st July 1973 the centenary of the opening of the Peel line was marked by a special train on the Port Erin line, which celebrated its own centenary in style the following year. On the 1st August 1974 No.4 Loch, also celebrating 100 years and having completed 2,000,000 miles, hauled a special train from Douglas, stopping at every station to pick up guests to attend a fete in Port Erin.

Tynwald debated the future of the line in 1974 and, after much discussion, the railway company was offered assistance to run four trains daily except Saturdays, between Port Erin and Castletown from 1975 onwards. These were extended to Ballasalla in 1976, efforts then being concentrated on a return to Douglas, still the main tourist centre. Government approval came in 1977, the same year as the Manx Electric returned to Ramsey, so the entire Port Erin line was open once again.

The Government was persuaded to purchase the line in 1977, following the election of several new members of Tynwald at the Manx general election of 1976. The steam railway became part of the Manx Electric Railway Board's responsibility, under the title 'Isle of Man Railways'.

The canopies at Douglas station were removed and Port Soderick station building was sold, as part of a drive to reduce costs and tidy up the railway. Douglas station also lost its signals and the 11 tracks were reduced to five to reduce loan costs. At Ballasalla, surplus land was sold for office development in return for a new station building on the other side of the line. Santa specials were introduced and now form an important part of the railway calendar. New boilers were obtained for Nos.11 and 12, extensive track repairs carried out and coaches renovated.

In 1983 the Manx Electric Railway Board became The Isle of Man Passenger Transport Board and this in turn became part of the Department of Tourism and Transport in 1986.

Plans for the 1993 'Year of Railways' included an attempt to bring an American Baldwin 4-4-0 to the line but sadly this did not come about. The day before the official launch of the year of railways, No.17 was named Viking at Douglas station. The county Donegal railcars were giving rides around Douglas station to a group of Irish railfans.

No.4 Loch had a couple of visits to the Manx Electric during 1993 and spent the intervening time on its own line

An unidentified locomotive leads a four-coach train round the curve on the approach to Colby station. Unless requested to stop at Ballabeg the train will have run non stop from Castletown and no doubt got up some speed. The buildings in the background are on the A28 New Road that forms part of the Southern 100 race circuit.

The Colby station building was originally located at Braddan, recent attention and repair means it looks as good as new.

One of the containers used in an experiment to increase revenue is preserved, although in need of attention, at Ballabeg station.

No.12 Hutchinson gets ready to depart from Ballabeg station with a Port Erin bound train. Pictures taken at this station have featured on numerous publicity features for the railway. The varying height of the coach stock is clearly evident from this view.

No.12 again, this time running bunker first towards Douglas round the curve that brings the line parallel with the Castletown bypass road, adjacent to the start/finish point for the Southern race circuit. During racing the railway provides a special service linking Castletown with the south of the Island, the road diversions being unsuitable for buses!

About to pass beneath the Malew Road, again part of the racing circuit, No.11 Maitland approaches Castletown with a Douglas bound train on the 2nd June 2006. The superb new trackwork is clearly evident in this view.

The 2009 season must have been one of the wettest the author can remember! Needless to say, when the weather was suitable, the opportunity was taken to get out with the camera. Such was the case on the 27th June when locomotive No.13 Kissack was captured departing from Castletown with the 12.20 from Douglas to Port Erin.

On the 24th July 2006 an evening special operated as far as Castletown hauled by former Manx Northern Railway locomotive No.4, that became No.15 in the IOMR fleet. The locomotive was unusually on the track, chimney facing Douglas and so makes an unusual picture whilst awaiting departure from Castletown at just before 20.00.

facing the 'wrong way', ie facing Douglas instead of Port Erin.

One of the highlights of the year was the return to service on the 20th June of No.10 G. H. Wood, using the boiler of No.13 Kissack and painted in an attractive Brunswick Green livery. Locomotive No.6 Peveril was cosmetically restored by the IOMSRSA.

Two accidents marred 1993, on the 4th June No.11 collided with a Metro car on the crossing at White Hoe. The car, driven by a district nurse was pushed 40 yards along the track by the train but although having to be cut free the nurse was not seriously injured. A second incident occurred between Ballabeg and Colby when a tractor and trailer were in collision, again with loco No.11. The locomotive sustained minimal damage while some damage was caused to grab rails on the coaches as they brushed past the road trailer whilst the train came to a stop.

The Duchess of Kent travelled from Douglas to Port Erin on the 22nd September with a stop at Ballasalla for refreshments, the train using F45, 36 and 29 and hauled by locomotive No.10.

New crossing lights were installed at Ballasalla and the station trackwork was relaid during the winter of 1993/94, as was most of the line between Port Erin and Port St. Mary. The wooden canopy at Castletown was demolished during the restoration of the brick building. Level crossing lights were also installed at White Hoe following the incident earlier in the year.

The success of the 'Year of Railways' led to ideas being collated for the forthcoming Snaefell Mountain Railway centenary in 1995. Former MNR locomotive No.15 Caledonia was removed from Port Erin Museum for inspection and possible return to steam for the 1995 season.

The Caledonia made a triumphant return to steam in time for the 1995 season, the highlight being its return to the Snaefell line, operating on a specially laid 3'0" section between Bungalow and the Summit with Manx Electric trailers 57 and 58. The locomotive made an impressive sight on the Island's highest mountain.

Shortly after the close of the 1995 season a special train was operated for the emergency services into the Nunnery cutting for a simulated car collision in the deep cutting. No.10 and four coaches made up the collision train while No.17 and a flat were used as an ambulance train to bring

Having travelled on the first northbound train of the 2008 season and alighted at Castletown, the Author awaited the arrival of the first southbound service. Duly captured by the camera, No.13 Kissack arrives at Castletown on a fine spring day. Poulson Park is visible behind the train.

In the late afternoon sun of an early November day, No.10 G. H. Wood approaches Castletown station and is about to pass under the bridge at the Douglas end of the station. The houses of Brookfield Avenue form the backdrop.

On a bright June morning, No.10 G. H. Wood storms past Ronaldsway Halt with the 07.45 commuter service to Douglas. The Ronaldsway Industrial Estate is to the left of the train, the early arrivals there no doubt surprised by the train passing at just after 08.00.

Another view at Ronaldsway Halt, this time of a southbound train with No.13 Kissack in charge. The public footpath crosses the line at this point and makes a pleasant walk to either Castletown or Ballasalla.

On the same evening as the picture on page 24 No.15 Caledonia trundles through Ronaldsway Halt, the short platform visible beside the locomotive. Ronaldsway airport is just a few minutes walk from here making it possible to travel to the airport by train.

On a sunny 2nd June 2006, No.4 Loch is gently letting off steam as she approaches Ronaldsway Halt with the early afternoon train from Douglas. The five-coach train would be necessary as the annual TT festival is on and many of the bikers enjoy a ride on the railway during their visit.

Having left the housing estates of Ballasalla the line emerges to run alongside the Silverburn River. No.10 G. H. Wood makes a fine sight framed among the trees as it heads south with the late afternoon service on the 3rd June 2006. The next scheduled stop will be Castletown.

Immediately at the southern end of Ballasalla station the line crosses the main A5 Douglas to South road. No.10 G. H. Wood makes a steady departure from the station while the passenger from the white van the other side of the crossing takes advantage of the situation to grab a picture of the passing train. The lifting barriers were installed as part of the IRIS scheme relay.

During normal timetable operation the north and southbound trains pass at Ballasalla. Here No.8 Fenella arrives with the northbound train. The close proximity of the level crossing is evident from this picture as the third and fourth coaches are still crossing the road.

out the wounded.

During the 1995/96 winter Tynwald approved the building of a new transport headquarters at Banks Circus adjacent to the railway station in Douglas. The development that would include a new bus maintenance facility to replace the existing one at Homefield would require the station signal box to be moved from its original position and the demolition of the former Mirn & Co. carriage shed, the last survivor of the three originally built to serve the railway. Work on the signal box move and demolition of the shed was expected to be completed in time for the new building to be started early in 1997.

Following the success of the reinstatement of the Caledonia, plans for the 125th anniversary of the opening of the Douglas to Peel line in 1998 began to include the return to steam of locomotive No.1 Sutherland. With this in mind the locomotive was removed from the Port Erin Museum in October 1996 and towed to Douglas.

The body of coach F57 was scrapped creating an additional flat runner, while No.4 Loch was withdrawn from service pending a full overhaul at the end of the 1996 season.

A batch of second-hand wagons from the Lochaber

Railway at Fort William were acquired for use on the line, to augment the existing permanent way fleet.

A series of speed restrictions were imposed for the 1997 running season, a high number of broken spring incidents occurring as a result of the poor track.

A major rebuild and refurbishment project for the Port Erin Museum began in 1997 with the framework being stripped of its old cladding. The former locomotive shed was returned to its proper use and the goods shed, used as a locomotive shed in recent years was incorporated into the new museum. The water tower was also rebuilt.

Partial height platforms were installed at Castletown station during 1997/98, although preliminary work had begun the previous winter.

Douglas station was completely relaid during the winter, using new rail, sleepers and ballast, partly in preparation for the building of the new integrated bus parking, workshops and transport headquarters.

In order to replace the old carriage shed, the Government advertised for expressions of interest from contractors to build two new sheds, one at Douglas and the other at Port Erin. It was also planned to fill the 'Gap' between the existing locomotive sheds and

The spring sunshine catches the side of coach F54, a complete rebuild, as it departs from Ballasalla hauled by No.4 Loch with the last train of the day on just the second day of the 2008 season.

A busy scene at Ballasalla station on a dampish day in June 2007. Nos.8 and 13 have arrived with the last southbound train and No.8 has uncoupled and moved forward. The gap between those tow locomotives frames No.4 arriving with the northbound train. No.8 then shunted onto the back of the northbound train, No.13 departed for Port Erin, Nos.4 and 8 pulling and pushing the Douglas bound train.

An unusual picture of what appears to be a southbound train in the northbound platform but, alas not. On the other end of the seven coach train is No.4 Loch and the pair are awaiting the off and departure to Douglas. It is TT Mad Sunday and so the trains enjoy full loads, in particular when rain and mist have closed much of the mountain racing circuit.

During normal operation the two trains pass at Ballasalla. On a bright sunny day the driver of the northbound train hauled by No.12 Hutchinson is about to hand over the single line 'Staff' or 'Ticket' to the driver of No.10 G. H. Wood operating the Port Erin bound train. The Staff is necessary to prevent two trains being on the same section of line at the same time. Only when the driver has the Staff in his possession, may he proceed.

Ballahick crossing is situated just a few hundred yards away on the Douglas side of Ballasalla station. Here with a good head of steam is No.4 Loch approaching the crossing with a southbound train. The houses visible to the left of the train are in Ballabridson Park.

During June 2007 the Author was treated to a footplate trip from Port Erin to Douglas and back. Needless to say the camera travelled as well! Captured from the footplate of No.13 Kissack is No.4 Loch arriving at Ballasalla with the first train of the day.

Ballabridson Park leads down to the line at one place and provides this vantage point of an approaching train. Captured using a telephoto lens, No.4 Loch approaches Ballasalla with a southbound train on Sunday the 11th May 2008.

No.13 Kissack at speed in the countryside. The derelict building visible over and to the left of the locomotive is what remains of Ballawoods crossing keeper's cottage. Like all other crossings on the line it is now automatic with lifting gates. The run from here to Ballasalla is downhill so little steam will be required.

paintshop/carriage works to provide yet more undercover storage.

Also announced at the end of November was the plan to restore the two former County Donegal railcars and expressions of interest were once again invited from potential contractors.

Work on the Castletown platforms continued and was completed by the beginning of the 1998 season.

Meanwhile in the sheds, work on the rebuild of locomotive No.1 was progressing well, while during March 1998 No.4 was loaded onto a lorry and taken to Laxey for some track tests. On its return to Douglas a unique photographic opportunity was created at the Sea Terminal with the locomotive being posed alongside the world record holding car Thrust SSC, that was making a brief publicity trip to the Island.

The mainland group of the IOMSRSA completed the construction of a replica M wagon numbered M79 and announced the intention to build a replica H type as well. Indications began to emerge that there was an intention to repaint the coaching stock into red and cream livery.

The restored locomotive No.1 Sutherland, with boiler from No.8 was officially inaugurated at Douglas on the 2nd

May. The 125th anniversary of the opening of the Douglas to Peel line was celebrated on the 1st July when after a short ceremony, No.1 departed for Port Erin with a nine-coach train banked by No.11.

The IOMSRSA officially handed over the replica M wagon and announced that it had entered into a 21-year lease agreement to raise £30,000 to restore No.4 Loch to working condition. No.9 Douglas was the subject of a similar appeal in 1977 but the Government takeover thwarted the attempt and it was sold to a rival group.

The railcar restoration was well under way. The body of No.19 had been dismantled while that of 20 was being used to create working drawings for the rebuild of both cars.

Peel saw its first steam locomotive for 30 years on the 8th July when No.1 was transported by road to the city and operated on a short demonstration track laid in the car park of the Manx National Heritage House of Mannanan. The loco returned to Peel on the 22nd August. On one of the return road trips to Douglas, the opportunity was taken to visit the St. John's station site and to pose the loco on its road trailer under the bridge that carried the Foxdale line over the main line to the east of the station.

Construction of the new carriage sheds had continued

No.13 Kissack in charge of the northbound TT commuter service during the 2008 festival. The train has just passed Ballawoods crossing and is now in open countryside before reaching Blackboards. The first coach is F45, pressed into service before its repaint was completed, hence the grey undercoated end nearest the locomotive.

At the end of the first week of the 2009 season, locomotive No.10 G. H. Wood is caught by the camera as it passes Ballaquaggan farm with the last train of the day for Douglas. Its Easter Sunday the 12th April and the passenger loads made the use of six coaches necessary.

A spot known locally as Blackboards with No.8 Fenella heading a southbound train. It is about to pass beneath the main Douglas to south road that is also visible to the right of the train. The bridge under which the train is about to pass has often been damaged by vehicles that fail to make it round the sharp bend in the road.

Shortly before reaching Blackboards, southbound trains are visible from the main road across a field. No.10 G. H. Wood, before being repainted green, is captured with a neat four-coach train during June 2006.

To the west of Santon station the line turns left and then continues towards Blackboards and the south. Here we see No.11 Maitland with a heavy five-coach northbound train. The locomotive is about to cross a bridge over Santon Burn while the buildings just visible at the top of the picture are at Cooilcam. The driver will be sounding his whistle to alert any intending passengers at Santon of his approach.

Santon station is perhaps the most picturesque on the line. No.4 Loch has just picked up some passengers and is about to depart for the south with a lengthy train. The palm trees make an interesting backdrop to the picture.

Santon gets renamed Santa's Halt for one weekend each December and the station building turned into a grotto. Train loads of excited children, and adults!, arrive by steam train to visit Santa.

through the summer, that at Douglas was first used just after the Santa train weekend at the end of 1998. The Port Erin shed was a week or so behind and had its first occupants on the 16th December. The red and cream livery did not materialize for 1998.

Coach F21 was repatriated from the Cavan and Leitrim railway in Ireland. The relocation of the Douglas signal box was completed by the beginning of the 1999 season, a new set of steps were provided and the main structure was refurbished and fully repainted. Completion of the new sheds allowed demolition of the old one to take place between the 6th and 8th June 1999.

The 125th anniversary of the south line was celebrated

timetable required trains to pass at Santon and as a consequence a stationmaster was employed. It also became a base for the permanent way gang.

Work on the rebuild of the Donegal railcars was halted after a considerable overrun on cost and still there was a great deal of work to do. Meanwhile fully rebuilt F54 returned to service on the 9th March, a tribute to the talent of the railway craftsman involved.

The body of former Manx Northern Railway coach N41 was removed from its long-term home outside the Douglas

No.4 Loch at speed approaching the A25 Old Castletown Road bridge and beginning a long straight run before making the approach to Santon Station on the 3rd June 2006. The train is just about five miles from Douglas.

The chassis of coach F70 has been converted into this twin ballast hopper and carries the number 2. It is seen here resting in the siding at Santon station.

with a special train on the 1st August 1999 and the official opening of the new museum adjacent to Port Erin Station.

The Steam Railway provided, as did several places on the Island, location for the filming of the new 'Thomas and the Magic Railroad' during 1999. Castletown station was clad in timber and renamed Shining Time, while the goods shed at Port St. Mary was used for indoor work and had a wooden extension added at one end.

The line entered its third century as the year 2000 dawned and was treated to a new timetable for the summer with six trains each way during the peak season and the normal four train off peak service times changed to allow longer days in Douglas and Port Erin. In a break with recent tradition, trains passed at Castletown instead of Ballasalla.

Santon station had become the latest to receive half-height platforms during the 1999/2000 winter. The 2000

shed and put in store in early May. New mess facilities for the train crews were provided by a portable cabin nearby. Meanwhile the body of C1 (part of F64) was moved from storage at Douglas to Peel in June 2001 for display alongside the former water tower and restoration by Peel Heritage Trust who look after the whole display area.

Following restoration at the Ramsey Shipyard, van Gr12 was moved to display adjacent to the former Lezayre station, itself also restored, while the replica H wagon was completed by the July of 2000.

No.1 Sutherland was repainted into the now standard Indian red livery during the latter part of 2000 and the bodies were removed from coaches F41 and F70.

HRH Prince Edward and his royal party travelled from Douglas to Santon to attend the Santon Fayre on the 7th July 2001.

Plans were unveiled by the Department of Transport to make improvements to the road at Kewaigue, involving the

The main processing works associated with the all Island sewage system is at Meary Veg, the access road crossing the railway by way of a new bridge. Captured from the bridge during National week 2006 is No.13 Kissack, emerging from Crogga woods and heading south with the last train of the day.

construction of a new bridge to the Douglas end of the existing one and with greater clearance for high road vehicles.

Following an agreement between the IOMSRSA and Isle of Man Transport, No.4 Loch left the Island on the 6th March 2001 for Chatham Steam, where a full overhaul took place, including a new boiler.

The access road to the new IRIS sewage processing plant at Meary Veg required a new bridge over the line just south of the Crogga woods. The bridge built of concrete and faced with stone was due for completion by August 2001.

The 2001 season drew to a close on the 28th October with the last trains running very full. Just about every local enthusiast and a large contingent of interested residents and no doubt a few visitors took the opportunity of one last complete trip before the end of the season, the last complete trips until the start of the 2004 season.

The reason for this was once again the IRIS scheme. A new underground pipeline was to be laid along the length of the line from Meary Veg to Port Erin over the next two years, with the steam railway only operating over part of its length.

On the last day the 14.00 from Douglas and the 16.35

return carried a commorative headboard marking the retirement of long-standing driver John Elkin. John was due to retire before the complete line would reopen and so this would be his last ever complete trip as a driver.

No.1 Sutherland was in steam for the Santa weekend on the 8th and 9th December, the 9th was expected to be the last day it would be seen in steam prior to the boiler being returned to No.8, that was away at RMS Locotec for rebuilding.

Ballasalla received a full-height platform on the Douglas side to match that on the Port Erin side built in 1985. Bus-style shelters installed on the Douglas side at Castletown and Ballasalla and a new wooden one at Port Soderick all provided an improved ambience for the passengers.

Immediately after the last train of 2001 the track between Meary Veg and Santon station was lifted in preparation for the laying of the new pipeline. This short stretch needed to be finished in time for the start of the 2002 season. With the pipe laid, the track reinstated using completely new materials and testing completed, this length of line reopened as planned on the 15th April 2002.

The 2002 timetable was for trains between Douglas and Santon and between Castletown and Port Erin, with a

Although taken from just about the same spot, the different angle gives a completely different picture. Operating one of the 2008 Santa trains and with frost still on the ground, No.10 G. H. Wood, complete with face and Christmas headboard, makes a fine sight as she climbs the bank with five coaches in tow.

The station building at Port Soderick is now a private residence and is just visible to the left of this picture. No.4 Loch pauses with a southbound train on 7th October 2006. The track through the station has since been completely relaid.

Despite the provision of a passing loop it is rare for trains to actually pass at Port Soderick. However, during the 2008 Santa Train operation, trains did pass at the station. Here No.13 Kissack, complete with face and 'Merry Christmas' headboard awaits departure with a southbound train while a northbound train is in the adjacent platform.

During the 1998 'Steam 125' celebrations, Manx Electric car No.33 operated a number of specials on the steam railway, the electric power coming from a generator mounted on an MER wagon with a van body built over it to disguise its purpose. MER car 33 is seen at Port Soderick with the van visible behind and Steam Railway locomotive No.17 Viking behind, about to perform the complicated reversing procedure, in readiness for the trams return to Douglas.

Most pictures at Keristal are taken from the seaward side of the line because even the last scheduled train is too early for the sun to have moved round far enough to light the train from the landward side. However, during the TT commuter train operations, the later departure from Douglas made this possible. With Coolebagad point visible to the right of the picture, No.12 Hutchinson heads towards Port Soderick with the evening commuter service on the 29th May 2008.

The rolls of straw in the harvested field date this picture to the late season as No.8 Fenella leads a three-coach train south towards Port Erin. The locomotive will still be working reasonably hard at this point, before shutting off for the next station stop at Port Soderick.

No.4 Loch emerging onto the bank above Port Soderick Glen and beginning perhaps the most scenic section of the line along the coast at Keristal.

connecting bus service linking the two parts. Two new water towers had to be constructed to accommodate the 2002 timetable, one at Santon and one at Castletown.

A severe storm on the night of the 21st October caused major problems on the east coast of the Island and some damage to the line between Douglas and Santon, with the result that this section did not reopen for the rest of the season.

No.1 Sutherland remained in service throughout the 2002 season, the work to remove the boiler and return it to No.8 was by then expected over the 2002/03 winter.

The IRIS work on the section between Santon and Castletown was completed on schedule, including the installation of automatic crossing barriers at most of the level crossings. These did cause a few problems in the early weeks

During the 1998 'Steam 125' celebrations, a number of demonstration freight trains were operated for the benefit of the many hundreds of photographers who travelled to the Island. On one such occasion No.1 Sutherland heads past Keristal with a mixed freight comprising a former coach chassis 'Flat' Gr12, M78 and a brake coach to provide accommodation for the guard.

of the 2003 timetable. With the northern section completed, the IRIS scheme moved to the southern section. Trains operated between Douglas and Castletown and between Port St. Mary and Port Erin for the 2003 season with the connecting bus service between the two.

A full-scale study into the provision of commuter trains was undertaken but concluded that at the time such a service was not viable. An interesting point here is that the vast majority of those who drive to work in Douglas actually park their car further from their office than the distance to the railway station!

Port Soderick gained a second full-height platform during early 2003, as did Ronaldsway Halt.

Locomotive No.8 Fenella was finally re-inaugurated on Friday the 5th September 2003 in a short ceremony at Douglas station.

The IRIS pipeline laying on the southern section went to plan, the new trackwork arriving on the Island during the 2003 season and the relay starting around the end of the season.

A number of contractors wagons and a Hunslett 3'0" gauge locomotive, now No.18 Ailsa, were used during the relay work. Further automated level crossings were installed, the whole project being completed in time, or almost, for the

Another of the attractions for the 1998 season, was the turning round of No.4 Loch, so that it faced Douglas. This allowed this unusual view of No.11 Maitland and No.4 double heading a southbound train, also captured in the Keristal area.

start of the new season, delayed until Monday the 3rd May, a date that marked another milestone in the long history of the railway.

Additional work was completed at Ronaldsway Halt to improve the platform with the installation of a wooden platform edge, while Colby received full-height platforms on both tracks and the former Braddan station building was refurbished and repainted.

After two years of curtailed running, the steam railway returned to its full length for the 2004 season, with the now standard four-train service operating in each direction and passing at Ballasalla, not at Castletown as had been the case for a short while. Many mourned the loss of the rattle and roll but the new track gives the line a whole new lease of life.

The colour light starter signals at the end of the Douglas platforms were replaced by more authentic semaphore ones

The Isle of Man has an abundance of Gorse and in the spring, this provides a good splash of colour to wide areas of the Island. With just a three-coach train, No.4 Loch is about to start the long descent into Douglas as it runs along high above the Irish Sea at Keristal.

Another view of No.4 Loch steaming along at Keristal with the last train of the day for Port Erin. It's early September and on a clear day the passengers would be able to look back beyond the headland to the hills of the English Lake District.

In early June 2006 an unidentified locomotive takes the first Douglas bound train of the day past Ellenbrook. The five coaches are likely to be full of motorcycle enthusiasts visiting the Island for the annual TT races.

at the beginning of the 2005 season.

During the race periods on the Southern 100 circuit and the consequential suspension of through bus services, a special train was operated from Port Erin to Castletown and back to convey some of the stranded commuters.

On Monday the 25th July 2005 a short ceremony was held at Douglas station to officially name recently acquired Hunslett diesel, numbered 18 in the fleet. The name Ailsa, kept secret until the day, was unveiled by Mr Cecil Mitchell, a Ballasalla resident who celebrated his 100th birthday that year. Mr Mitchell was then photographed alongside locomotives Nos. 10 and 11 both of which were also celebrating their 100th birthdays.

A crack in the IRIS pipeline at the northern end of Castletown station caused no disruption to services despite the digging of a large hole to access the pipeline.

A Samaritans Christmas Child 'Shoebox' campaign special train operated from Port Erin to Douglas on Tuesday the 1st November 2005, a couple of days after the end of the season services that had produced 143,736 passengers, up from 140,499 the year before.

The line received a top 10 place in the National newspaper 'The Independent' Top 10 best car-free days out, beating the likes of the Orient Express in the process.

During the winter of 2005/06 winter the track was relaid

between Meary Veg and a point just south of Port Soderick station. Various problems with the automatic crossing barriers at the beginning of the season were swiftly attended to. No.4 Loch returned to service at the beginning of the 2006 season.

Sadness swept through the entire staff of Isle of Man Transport on the 2nd August 2006 with the news of the death of Assistant Engineer Colin Goldsmith. On the day of his funeral the 10th August, the trains on the steam railway carried wreaths in memory of Colin.

The Shoebox special operated again on the 7th November 2006.

Work over the 2006/07 winter included the complete relay of Port Soderick station, joining up with the earlier relay through Crogga woods to Meary Veg. New tastefully produced enamelled metal signs were installed above the doors in all the rolling stock, warning of the dangers of leaning out.

The same four-train service was in the timetable for 2007. Locomotive No.10 G. H. Wood was repainted into Ailsa green livery and had the honour of hauling the railway's first commuter train for many years, when during the TT fortnight an 07.45 train operated from Port Erin to Douglas with a 17.30 return. A special commuter ticket was available but regrettably very few people used the service.

The 40th anniversary of the beginning of the important Ailsa period was marked by a short ceremony at Douglas but sadly No.10 had failed and was only able to take part as a static exhibit.

Congestion on the approaches to Douglas during the rush hour periods led to the call for the two former County Donegal railcars to be completed and operated as a commuter service. It got no further but there are still efforts to find a way forward, possibly using some external funding and/or manpower.

Santon and Ballasalla stations were repainted in the standard red and cream colours over the winter. At Castletown some work was carried out on the former goods shed, including the removal of a large wooden advertising board, thus revealing more of the building's stonework. At Port Erin, two of the level crossing gates have been replaced with wooden ones, which look far more in place than the old metal ones.

Following the end of the season, the now annual 'Shoebox' train operated on the 6th November and the Santa trains over the weekend of 8th and 9th December.

The 2008 season started as usual at Easter and was not affected by the safety issues on the Manx Electric.

The TT trains were repeated, indeed they appeared in the annual timetable leaflet, this time with some reduced fares and the availability of Manx12 bus tickets and residents tickets, resulting in far more commuter passengers being carried.

The beginning of the 2009 season has witnessed some good passenger loads, necessitating the need for up to six-coach trains on occasions. Shortly before the services started it was announced, that from the end of September until the end of the season in early November, only one train will operate thus reducing the service to two trains each way each day.

A welcome addition from earlier in the year was the re-instatement of mileposts along the line, the last of the previous posts were lost in the major relay in the early 2000s.

During the season a new Director of Public Transport was appointed and some interesting initiatives followed. On the eve of the last day of the season a Hop-tu-Naa train ran from Douglas to Castletown, the 240 passengers then enjoying a ghost walk around the town before the journey back to Douglas and a hotpot supper.

The Santa trains were such a success that four additional trains ran the following weekend and a 'Blow away the Cobwebs' special on the 30th December carried a full load of passengers.

The 2010 season dates were announced and show services starting on the 13th March, some two weeks earlier than might have been expected.

The old and the new. During the early 2000s the A6 road from Spring Valley into south Douglas was upgraded to encourage better use by commuters from the south, thus reducing the congestion at Quarter Bridge. No.13 Kissack has crossed the new road bridge and is on the old, now disused, bridge on its way south with the first train of the day on the 2nd July 2006. It's National week and the appropriate headboard is carried.

On the 3rd June 2008 the first train of the day has arrived at Douglas behind No.12 Hutchinson. The large number of passengers is typical of the loads carried during the TT festivals. It's the Tuesday of race week, there is no racing so many of the visitors let the train take the strain.

Running round the train after arrival at Douglas. Many thousands of pictures are taken of the locomotives at this point, captured by the passengers as they walk off the platform. No.13 has just completed it journey from Port Erin. Driver Tommy Brown gives a friendly smile and is no doubt thinking about a good cup of tea!

The final day of operation for the season was Sunday 1st November. The last train left Port Erin at 16.20 and so arrived at Douglas 'after dark'. Locomotive No.10 G H Wood is seen at journeys end, complete with headlight. Passengers had disembarked and the crew were preparing to shunt the coaches into the shed for the winter. The blurring of the clouds indicates that it was a windy night.

An arriving passenger's view of a train ready for departure from Douglas. With just a few minutes to go before departure, No.4 Loch provides a smokey atmosphere over the station. The 4.15pm to Port Erin will soon be underway, the young enthusiast on board and enjoying his journey.

A view of the superb semaphore signals that recently replaced the colour light ones on the end of the Douglas platforms.

Nº 4

Caution
C.C.T.V.
in
operation

Isle of Man
transport
arraghey ellan vannin

DO NOT
TRESPASS
ON THE
RAILWAY

Below Left: Every year the railway run a 'Thomas the Tank' weekend, encouraging the younger generation to come and enjoy the railway. No.15 Caledonia is in charge of the 'Troubesome Trucks' M78 and H1. The two trucks are adorned with faces and fitted with benches and operate short trips up the line. The trio are nearly ready for departure from Douglas.

Below: Coal is only available at Douglas, apart from small emergency supplies, thus it is necessary to ensure that enough coal is available for the return trip to Port Erin. Reloading after arrival with the first train of the day, fireman Rodney Swift burns off the breakfast calories.

Above: No.13 Kissack keeps company with one of the Simplex diesels at Douglas shed, after arriving with the first train of the day. Driver John Smith, who is also the Stationmaster at Castletown looks on.

Recently rebuilt former Manx Northern Railway van Gr12 is captured by the camera outside the Douglas shed complex. The van was built in 1879 and was No.15 in the Manx Northern Railway fleet.

Above: Supplies of oil are also stored at Douglas. Driver John Smith replenishes his stocks before departing for Port Erin.

Below Left: Nos.5 Mona and 6 Peveril languish in the back corner of the old carriage shed at Douglas. Shortly after this picture was taken, No.6 was removed from here and cosmetically restored by the Isle of Man Steam Railway Supporters' Association and is now on display in the museum at Port Erin. No.5 is still stored. Below Right: The railway engineering staff undertake all but the very major overhaul of the locomotives and rolling stock. Here No.12 Hutchinson is stripped down for overhaul inside the Douglas workshops.

Below: Brake coach F49 undergoing attention in the Douglas workshops. The refurbished bogie can be seen to the left of the picture, ready to be placed back under the coach and re-enter service..

Below: During an evening photographic session, locomotives Nos.10 and 15 G. H. Wood and Caledonia pose in the station.

Former County Donegal railcars Nos.19 and 20 attract plenty of attention from the photographers.

One of the Wickham railcars stands outside the workshop.

Below Left: The two County Donegal railcars in the workshops during their protracted rebuild. The cars remain in just about this state some 10 years after the project was started. Below Right: The signal box is captured during its journey across the former goods yard from its original position adjacent to the old carriage shed, to its current position. The old carriage shed is visible behind.

Below: The new carriage shed under construction, the finished shed providing a somewhat better environment than the one it replaced.

Below: The Jackson built tamping machine tucked away in the locomotive shed for the summer. During each winter this machine will be out, busy checking the trackwork across the steam and Manx Electric systems.

As part of the 1998 'Steam125' Celebrations locomotive No. 1 Sutherland, was returned to steam. On two occasions No.1 was taken to Peel and placed on a short length of demonstration track in the House of Mannanan car park. Would this be the last time a steam locomotive makes it to Peel, lets hope not.

Diesel locomotive No.18 Ailsa is seen at Santon with a short works train comprising of the well wagon with hedge cutting tractor and ballast wagon. This locomotive was brought to the Island by the contractor responsible for the IRIS relay scheme and was originally from the Channel Tunnel construction fleet.

Below: A rare picture of locomotive No.2 Derby at an unidentified location with a short train comprising of van E1 and two bogie coaches. No.2 was withdrawn and dismantled in 1951, only the front pony truck survives. Notice the lack of locomotive number on the bunker end.

Below: A recently discovered postcard view of Port Erin station with two lengthy trains in adjacent platforms. The impressive gates onto the platform have gone and there is a distinct lack of buildings visible into the distance. The houses in Droghadfayle Road were built in the early 1930s dating this picture to the 1920s or earlier. The bay platform has been shortened to beyond the end of the right-hand train and the nearer end has been converted into a bus park

Below: A picture taken by the Author around 28 years ago shows the two former County Donegal Railway diesel railcars entering Castletown with a special service from Port Erin to Douglas.

Below: Another view of St. Johns station taken from the footbridge with No.14 Thornhill with a train for Ramsey on the left. Leaving St. John's, trains for Peel and Ramsey ran parallel for a while and often had a race to the point where they diverged.

A view of Peel station in 1947 with a train for Douglas in the right-hand platform and a couple of coaches in the far siding and an 'M' wagon in the siding. It is hard to believe that just 21 years later the last train operated from Peel and the station closed. The station building celebrated its centenary in 2008.

THE CROGGA VALLEY RAILWAY

The Isle of Man's newest passenger-carrying railway is situated in the grounds of Crogga, an impressive Victorian Estate. The 7¼" railway takes its name from the river that flows through the grounds and the valley in which it sits. It was never intended to be open to the public on a regular basis. Chris Beauman is the current owner.

The previous owner, Nick Dodson, had had a short 7¼" gauge railway round the garden of his home at Port-e-Vullen in the north of the Island. This was dismantled when he moved to Crogga.

Construction of the line began in 2001, the first task being to dig out and lay the concrete base for the locomotive shed, workshops and office. The main station and workshop area are adjacent to and visible from the Isle of Man Steam Railway between Port Soderick and Santon. Nick enlisted the help of Jack Dibnah, son of the Late Fred Dibnah to build the railway.

Following construction of the buildings, track was laid in the sheds and then outside, the whole station area being completed before the tracklaying began in the direction of the stable block situated adjacent to the Old Castletown Road.

The line eventually reached the main road at the side of the lake, and plans were made by Chris to bridge the river and extend into the wooded area on the other side of the lake. A runround loop was installed at the temporary terminus to allow trains to operate. Most of the pointwork was built on site by Jack, some however being bought in.

The forerunner to the Crogga Valley Railway was this private railway round a garden in Port e Vullen. Samastipur runs light engine with some superb coastline in the background..

The main station building on the railway overlooks the Isle of Man Steam Railway.

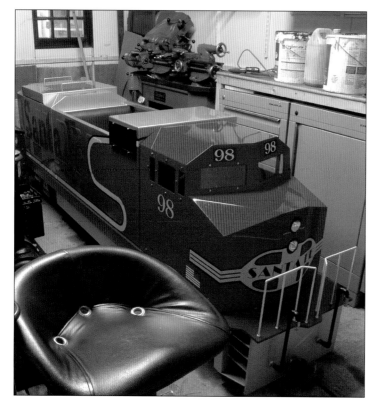

The locomotive shed with Santa Fe No.98 and a steam locomotive Romulus resting between duties. The workshops are well equipped to deal with all but the heaviest maintenance required.

Pullman lavatories on the Isle of Man. This facility is constructed and finished with surplus panelling and fittings from Pullman car Pegasus, built in 1951 for the famous Golden Arrow and now fully restored and part of the equally famous Orient Express.

The works diesel locomotive also having a day off.

Hiding in the nearby carriage shed is this under construction chassis for a Garrett style locomotive. Once completed this machine will be a spectacular sight operating on the line.

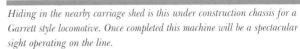

Below: The passenger rolling stock shares its shed with the Garrett chassis and a boat.

Below: Even a miniature railway needs a permanent way train. Here a couple of side tipping ballast wagons await their next duties. Their buckets have been turned over to prevent water collecting.

Above: A triple-header with Ardwhallin, Ramsey and Samastipur arriving at the main station during May 2005 as an Isle of Man Steam Railway train hauled by No.8 Fenella passes on its way to Douglas. (John Messenger)

Above: A lengthy train made up of a variety of rolling stock and hauled by Samastipur heads up the steep gradient towards the main station. The train is about to reach the passing loop. The line has yet to reach and cross the river feeding into the lake. (John Messenger)

A somewhat shorter train but with two locomotives rounds the curve. Looking up past the camera the passengers would have a super view of Crogga House. (John Messenger)

Two locomotives at what was the far end of the line before the completion of the bridge and extension to the other side of the lake. Ramsey and Ardwhallin await departure for the main station. (John Messenger)

Nick Dodson is the owner of several main line coaches including the Pullman car Pegasus, now a regular part of the Orient Express train. This vehicle had to be rebuilt and refurbished before it was allowed back on the main line. This rebuild left many original fittings spare and so the toilet and its panelling and fittings at Crogga all came from this now famous Pullman car.

An extension was planned to take the railway round the end of the lake through a short tunnel and into a new station. Groundwork was soon underway and the new station area was prepared for tracklaying. Former Isle of Man Railway sleepers were used to build a retaining wall to hold up the ground for the new station. A decking-style platform was constructed with steps down to a waterside deck and landing point.

A small locomotive and storage shed has been provided at the station that has three tracks and a traverser across the end to allow the release of the locomotive. The traversa is built using redundant equipment from mobile office racking.

The track was laid towards the site of the bridge that would take the line over the river that feeds into the lake adjacent to the Old Castletown Road. The bridge itself was constructed over the 2006/07 winter, the first train completing the ¼ mile journey during the summer of 2007. A canopy was added at the original station during 2007.

The passing loop below the stable block was removed and what was a siding higher up the lawns had become a passing loop. The steepest parts of the line have a gradient of 1 in 31.

Some sections of the straight track have been relaid using six-metre lengths rather than the four-metre lengths originally used. Points are controlled by conventional drop over levers and the line has yet to receive any signalling. All the sleepers and ballast have been sourced from supplies on the Island.

Plans for the future include the completion of the tunnel and extension of the line round the other end of the lake to rejoin the outward journey near the stable block. A turntable may be added using the remains of a bridge from the old line at Port-e-Vullen.

The railway has no resident steam locomotives at present but, an impressive Garrett-style locomotive is under construction based on an original built in 1909. A Santa Fe diesel locomotive was delivered new in 2005 from Knightley Light Railway, Nr Stafford, England and has Works No. 2212. There is also a small Lister locomotive supplied by L. A. Services Ltd, Bramcote, Warwickshire and several wagons.

The line looks set for a long future, possibly extended and perhaps one day, open to the public.

Santa Fe No.98 at the far end of the line, the station is situated above the lake and has its own station building that doubles as a Summerhouse. A traverser is installed at the end of the platform to transfer locomotives and stock from one track to another. (John Messenger)

CHAPTER THREE

THE DOUGLAS HORSE TRAMWAY

The Douglas Horse Tramway operates today on a 1.6 mile 3ft gauge track laid down the middle of the Promenade from Derby Castle at the northern end to the Sea Terminal at the southern end. The Tramway was first conceived in 1875 by Thomas Lightfoot, a retired civil engineer from Sheffield who was involved in the construction of the original Woodhead Tunnel, and later that year he lodged a proposal at the Rolls Office in Douglas. Spring 1876 saw an Act of Tynwald and the granting of Royal Assent for a tramway from Victoria Pier, part of the present sea terminal, to Summer Hill. The Act specified that only animal power could be used.

A single track line with passing loops was constructed with 35 lb/yd rail, the centre walkway for the horses being laid with small stones and tar. The Public Highway Surveyor inspected the line and it opened, without ceremony, between Summer Hill and the Iron Pier, situated opposite the bottom of Broadway, on the 7th August 1876.

The Starbuck Car & Wagon Co. Ltd, later G.F. Milnes & Co., delivered two double-deck tramcars, only one of which was actually operated on opening day, hauled by two horses.

The second stretch from the Iron Pier to Victoria Pier opened in January 1877. After experiments with just one horse, public opinion obliged the operators to continue to use two horses on the double-deck tramcars. Later that year the stable building that is still in use today was purchased to house the expanding stud of horses. In 1882 the Horse Tramway was sold to Isle of Man Tramway Ltd, which added two more passing loops in 1883, in order to increase service intervals to every 20 minutes. This was still insufficient and in 1884 a further passing loop was added and the tram fleet increased to eight.

Over 350,000 passengers enjoyed a ride on the line in 1885 and two more single-deck trams were added. Summer Hill terminus was rebuilt and renamed Derby Castle in 1886, permission being granted in the same year to double the track from Falcon Cliff to Derby Castle. Seventeen tramcars were now in the fleet and they all took part in the ceremony to mark the opening of the double-track section in 1887. In 1888 over half a million passengers were carried and 79,278 tram miles covered.

Twenty-six tramcars were in service by 1891 and all but a short stretch of line had been doubled. Thomas Lightfoot died on the 10th January 1893, just eight months before The Douglas & Laxey Coast Electric Tramway Co. opened the first stage of what is now the Manx Electric Railway, from Derby Castle to Groudle. The electric tramway terminus at Derby Castle, just 15ft away from the horse tram terminus, brought even more passengers to the Horse Tramway.

The Isle of Man Tramways & Electric Power Co. purchased the Horse Tramway for £38,000 in April 1894 in a deal that required them to construct a cable tramway to upper Douglas. In 1895 work commenced on the new tram depot at Derby Castle, which is still in use today. The offices on top were not added until 1935 and for a long time were home to what is now Isle of Man Transport. Since the latter's departure to Banks Circus a conference suite has been operated by Douglas Corporation. A cast-iron awning over the Horse Tramway terminal, sadly demolished as unsafe in 1980, was also built at this time.

Electrification of the tramway was considered by the Tramway Company in 1897 when, following completion of the last piece of double track, over one and a half million passengers were carried,

The Isle of Man Tramways & Electric Power Co. had been heavily reliant on Dumbells Bank to finance construction of the tramway and the Upper Douglas Cable Car System, so when Dumbells collapsed in 1900 the Tramway Company went into liquidation. In September 1901 the Manx Chancery accepted the £50,000 offer from Douglas Corporation for the Horse Tramway and cable car system. Thirty-six cars now operated on the Horse Tramway, 13 double-deckers, three single-deck saloons, 14 open toastracks and six roofed toastracks, motive power being provided by 68 horses. The electric tramway was sold in 1902 to a syndicate based in Manchester and later that year to the Manx Electric Railway Company.

In 1906 the Manx Electric Railway Company approached the corporation with the intent to electrify the Horse Tramway in order to provide a through service from Ramsey to Victoria Pier but this was again rejected, as was a further

The TT Bushy's tent, a regular TT attraction forms a backdrop for a Manx Telecom sponsored tram as it arrives at the Sea Terminal with a full load of visitors for the centenary TT Festival. Large numbers of motorcycle fans watch from the confines of the tent enclosure.

Nearing journeys end, car No.35 pulled by horse Ron, are captured while travelling along Loch Promenade opposite Victory House, a modern office block that now stands on the site of the former Villiers Hotel, on 29th May 2007..

Horse Nicola with Car No.37 in tow does battle with the traffic on Loch Promenade as she approaches the end of the line. One wonders if the engineers who constructed the tramway could ever imagined that the line would still be operating over 130 years later, and the vast amounts of traffic they have to encounter on each trip.

Douglas Corporation joined in the festive fun for Christmas 2009 by operating the very first Santa Horse Trams. Needless to say the event was a success and for the first day, Saturday the 19th December 2009, the weather was kind. Car No.1 was specially decorated for the event, fitted with an onboard generator, and is captured here passing Regent Street near the end of its journey along the Promenade. On return to Derby Castle the younger generation will visit Santa in his grotto.

During August 2003 horse Victor keeps up the pace with car No.38 as it passes the Methodist Church on Loch Promenade. Many of the former hotels along the Promenades have been demolished and replaced by residential apartment blocks. Loch Promenade has largely survived this redevelopment and retains many original buildings, thus giving an idea of what the entire route would have looked like half a century ago.

With the Promenade stretching away into the distance, Derby Castle is just off the right of the picture, horse John brings car No.33 past the Gaiety theatre and Sefton Hotel and begins the final section of the journey along Loch Promenade.

approach in 1908. Two more tramcars were delivered in 1907 and in 1909 it was ruled that a maximum of eight return journeys were to be operated by each horse in the course of a day.

During the First World War, a winter schedule operated, as the holiday industry slumped. However, by 1920 business was picking up again, with 44 cars available.

Motor buses were introduced along the Promenade for the first time in 1926 and it was proposed that they would eventually take over from the tramway. In 1927, after almost 50 years unbroken service, the tramway began closing for the winter.

Serious threats of closure were hanging over the line by 1933 but the Corporation embarked on a massive track relaying programme, using 65 lb/yd rail which would last 40 years, thus assuring the tramway of a future. Indeed, the Horse Tramway made a profit of £8,000 in 1933 compared with a loss of £4,280 on the bus services, a pattern that continued for several decades. Three more tramcars were added in 1935 and roller bearings were fitted to the existing fleet; the number of horses had reached 135.

The Second World War caused the tramway to close. All the horses were sold, the tramcars put into store, barbed wire erected between the tracks and many seafront hotels requisitioned for prisoners of war.

In April 1946, 42 horses arrived from Ireland, the tramcars emerged from store and a re-opening ceremony was performed on the 22nd May by Sir Geoffrey Bromet, the Lieutenant-Governor of the Island. A reduced service was operated but a profit still showed.

Holidaymakers poured back to the Island in 1947, tracklaying restarted and all looked good for the future until 1949, when it was suggested that open-top buses should replace the trams but fortunately the Corporation took no action in this direction. All but one of the double-deck cars had by now disappeared and in 1955 the sole survivor (No.14) left the Island for preservation in the Museum of British Transport at Clapham.

An anniversary parade was held in 1956 to mark 80 years of service, the horses and cars assembling at Victoria Pier before returning to Derby Castle in convoy.

Holiday traffic declined towards the end of the 1950s and threats of closure were again rumoured, but denied officially. Tynwald granted permission in 1961 for a fare increase, as the tramway was now regarded as a speciality ride. The Fleetwood steamer services ceased after the summer of 1961, resulting in a reduction in the number of day trippers to the Island in 1962.

Tynwald Day 1964 saw Her Majesty Queen Elizabeth, the Queen Mother, ride on specially prepared tram No.44 from Summer Hill to the Villa Marina. The stud of horses was 56 at the beginning of the year being reduced to 43 by the winter. Fifteen new horses were purchased at the beginning of 1965, a year that saw another Royal visit, this time by HRH Princess Margaret and Lord Snowdon.

A flat fare system was introduced in 1966 and the number of passengers showed an increase, which was to continue over the next few years.

HRH the Duke of Edinburgh visited the line in 1970, returning in 1972 with Her Majesty the Queen, HRH Princess Anne and Admiral of the Fleet, Earl Mountbatten of Burma. The Royal party rode from the new terminus at Victoria Pier to the Sefton Hotel in cars 44 and 36, both specially painted and decked out with flowers. The Promenade was crowded with a high percentage of the Islanders.

During the early 1970s the Isle of Man Tourist Board had been actively trying to increase the number of visitors to the Island through advertising, which in turn had increased the number of passengers on the Horse Tramway, and by 1973 the numbers were heading back up towards those of the early 1920s. In 1974 over one and a half million passengers were carried. The price of horses rose sharply during 1974/75 resulting in the Corporation deciding to start a breeding programme, new foals not working the tramway until they were at least three years old.

The centenary fell on the 7th August 1976 but as this was a Saturday the celebrations were held on Monday the 9th August, by chance during the author's first visit to the Island. The Science Museum in London, by now the home of double-decker No.14, was persuaded to allow it to return to the Island, be repainted and take part in the celebrations. Three other cars were also repainted including No.44 that was only returned to the depot the evening before. Stable staff worked through the night grooming the 50 horses, all brasswork was meticulously polished and nameboards provided for each horse.

At 10.00 the horses were led along the Promenade towards Victoria Pier where the trams were waiting, having been hauled there five at a time by a double-decker bus. Then at 11.15 the double-deck tram left Victoria Pier at the head of the procession that included the newly restored Upper Douglas cable car. Every serviceable tram followed, their passengers being issued with special centenary tickets. It is estimated that 30,000 people lined the Promenade from end to end.

The year 1979 was the millennium of Tynwald and after much promotion the number of visitors to the Island was

Captured from the balcony above the Villa Marina colonnade, Car No. 33 keeps up with horse John as the conductor collects fares from the few passengers travelling on the tram. The Islands war memorial is in the background.

The former Upper Douglas Cable Car system terminated at the junction of Broadway with the Promenade. Passing this junction is Car No.37 hauled by horse Gwynne on 3rd June 2008. In the distance to the right of the tram can be seen the white building with red doors that is the tramway depot at Derby Castle.

The balcony above the Castle Mona shops provides this vantage point, from where car No.37 with horse Nicola at the helm is captured heading towards the Sea Terminal on 28th June 2006. The promenade walkway to the right of the tram has been suggested as a possible relocation site for the trams, if it were deemed necessary to move them from the centre of the promenade.

Onchan Head and its golf course provide the backdrop to this view of car No.33 with horse Mark in charge heading south along the Promenade. Many passengers for the tramway arrive at Derby Castle on the Manx Electric Railway, the direction sign on the lamppost pointing towards the Electric Railway Terminus.

As an added attraction for the 2008 season, the Corporation re-introduced regular double deck tram operation along the tramway. A horse that wishes to remain anonymous hauls car No.18 past the Hilton Hotel bound for Derby Castle. This car has had an interesting life, built as a double decker, it was converted to single in the early 20th Century and back to double in 1988.

Passing the Hilton Hotel at speed, horse Mark has car No.33 in tow but sadly only a few passengers. The building at the top of the picture is the former Falcon Cliff Hotel, now offices. The hotel was served by the now derelict Falcon Cliff Lift, a single track funicular railway climbing up from behind the Hilton to just below the former hotel.

Below: On a damp 9th July 2008, horse Philip heads towards Derby Castle with car No.45. The crane in the background is on the site of the former Crescent leisure centre, now being converted into apartments incorporating the original facade of the leisure centre. The tram is passing a recently completed apartment block.

Shortly after passing the tramway stables, housed behind the white building visible to the immediate left of the tram, horse Michael enjoys the downward gradient and trots to keep clear of car 37 rolling along behind. Summerhill is seen climbing up to the right of the picture. In just a minute or so the tram will have reached the terminus.

A good illustration of the ease with which the horse is able to keep the tram moving along the Promenades. Although this section approaching the terminus is just downhill, the straps that join the horse to the tram are slack, indicating that the horse just needs to trot to keep ahead of the tram This is true for most of the journey, the effort from the horse is just to get the tram moving, then just needing to stay away from it.

Below: Another line of original buildings remains on Queens Promenade, the Rutland Hotel still open in a couple of them. Car No.33 with an unidentified horse make good progress towards the Derby Castle terminus. If the tram stops it is necessary for any traffic to stop behind the tram to allow passengers to board and alight safely.

Beginning a return trip along the Promenades is double deck car No.18 with an unidentified horse in control at the front. The conductor is seen issuing tickets on the upper deck. In order to reduce the weight for the horse, passengers are only carried on the upper deck of the tram.

The Horse Tramway motive power depot! Three of the horses keep a watchful eye on the Author during a visit to the stables in September 2008. The horses are extremely well looked after, each individual stable is large enough for the horse to lie down, plenty of food and water is always available and during the winter they are taken to graze in fields specially reserved for them on the outskirts of Douglas.

higher than in previous years and the tramway carried just over 860,000 passengers during the season.

The line made a loss in 1980 for the first time in its history, with passenger numbers down to 742,000, the beginning of what was to be a poor decade with numbers falling, apart from 1983 and 1987 that showed modest increases on the previous year. Total passengers for 1989 were down to 264,000 and by 1991 to just short of 180,000. Car No.46 spent the summer of 1987 on display in Nobles Park, Douglas before being shipped to the mainland, fully restored and displayed at the Woodside Ferry terminal, Birkenhead.

The 1993 season started earlier, at Easter, as part of the 'Year of Railways'. Fares for the year were £1.10 single or runabout, the ticket being valid for the whole day. Stored cars 11, 47 and 49 were moved from Ramsey MER car sheds to Douglas and placed behind the new steam railway carriage shed in June 1993. Cars 21 and 38 were repainted into a special blue and gold Douglas 2000 livery.

Mr Wilson Gibb retired as General Manager of the Horse Tramway on the 18th August 1993 and Mr Peter Cannan, who had worked on the tramway for 15 years, was appointed Tramway Supervisor. The celebrations for the Manx Electric and the resulting number of enthusiast visitors took the passenger figure back over the 200,000 mark for that year to 205,061.

Various suggestions regarding the future of the Horse Tramway were forthcoming, making it single track and/or moving it onto the Promenade walkway. These suggestions all formed part of a new Douglas 2000 project, looking at Douglas as it moved towards the 21st Century.

Car No.45 was returned to service in 1994 after a few years stored, the operating season reverting to early May through to the 1st October.

A safety drive by new management prevented conductors from riding on the front of the car, thus returning them to the rear platform from where they could observe any issues that arose with the passengers.

Cars 21 and 30 had their Douglas 2000 livery removed at the end of the 1995 season. During the 1995/96 winter the track at the Sea Terminal end of the line was lifted to allow work on the Island-wide IRIS sewage project to be undertaken. The track was back in place in good time for the commencement of the 1996 season.

The year of 1996 was the 120th birthday of the Horse Tramway and the centenary of Douglas Corporation; two trams, 36 and 43, appeared carrying illuminations celebrating the birthday.

Despite good loads in the early and mid evenings the overall Horse Tramway passenger numbers for the 1996

season were disappointing. The evening service proved very worthwhile and was complemented in the mid summer by the illuminated Manx Electric car working to Groudle in conjunction with the Groudle Glen Railway, enabling travel by horse, electric and steam all in one evening! The general appearance of the entire horse tram fleet was deemed to have improved under the recently appointed management.

Toastrack car No.40 was extensively rebuilt during the 1996/1997 winter and re-entered service on the 23rd July 1997. The all day ticket for the 1997 season was £1.40 and a four tram service was operated during the TT festival fortnight.

The oldest surviving car, No.11, was returned to Derby Castle in late 1998 with a plan for restoration to service condition.

In honour of the memory of Councillor John Harley, the Mayor of Douglas who died following an illness, the tramway and several other departments of the Corporation were closed from the 3rd to the 7th September 1999.

Just over a week later, on Friday the 17th September while travelling towards Derby Castle car 35 struck the counterweight of a lorry-mounted crane outside the new Tower Shopping Centre on Loch Promenade. Several passengers were injured, two requiring hospital treatment and the tram was badly damaged, the impact collapsing the roof onto the top of the seats.

Work to rebuild car 35 took place over the winter of 1999/2000, while along the route new red on white tram stop signs were installed. During the first half of 2000 the stables received a much needed upgrade. The traditional bays have been replaced with boxes, giving the horses room to lie down between shifts if they wish.

The 125th anniversary of the Horse Tramway was celebrated in 2001, each tram used in service that year receiving a special 125th logo sticker. On the evening of the actual anniversary, the 7th August, there was a parade with the Promenade closed to traffic to accommodate the large crowd that gathered. Unlike previous parades the start this time was at Derby Castle where the Mayor, Councillor Stephen Pitts, made his speech alongside the still to be restored car No.11. Double-deck car 18 led the cavalcade conveying the Lieutenant Governor Air Marshall Ian Macfadyen together with the visiting Governors of Jersey and Guernsey. Car 43 conveyed a party of visiting schoolchildren from the former Soviet Republic. On return to Derby Castle the party transferred to Summerland for a reception where a further speech was made by Betty Quirk, Chair of the Corporation Leisure and Services Committee.

A private car parked across the track on the approach to

On a wet July day, horse Albert arrives at Derby Castle with an empty tram from the Sea Terminal. Manx Electric car 22 and trailer can be seen behind the horse, awaiting departure for Laxey and Ramsey. Usually, the horse car would be bring intending passengers to the Manx Electric but, not today.

The tram horses are big strong animals. Here horse Philip stands proudly in front of car 35 awaiting departure from Derby Castle. An intending passenger purchases his ticket from the conductor.

Below: The two bays to the left of the depot feed into the tramway workshops. Car 40 stands outside whilst awaiting attention during the summer of 1996.

Below: Preserved Douglas Cable Car No.72/73 stands outside the horse tramway depot after a rare return trip along the Promenades. This tram was rebuilt and restored from the remains of two trams numbers 72 and 73 found in use as a residential dwelling in the north of the Island and made its first trip along the Promenades as part of the Horse Tramway centenary celebrations of 1976.

Below: For many years the tramway operated its own souvenir shop from converted tram No.22. The shop sold a wide range of tramway related gifts and souvenirs but sadly is no longer operational.

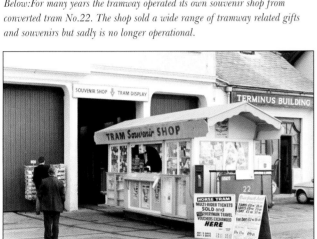

Below: This 1979 view shows Vulcan built horse car No.49 in use as a waiting room for Manx Electric passengers at Derby Castle. Built in 1935 at a cost of £520 the tram was one of three built by Vulcan that were capable of being operated as either closed or open cars with folding doors and seats.

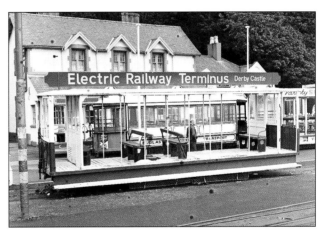

Car No.45 is seen during repainting and before the application of advertisement panels around the top of the body.

A visitors view of the tramway. Taken from a balcony room at the now Hilton Hotel on the Promenade, car 33 heads towards the Sea Terminal with a good load of passengers on a wet and miserable day.

Having a quiet day inside the tramway depot are winter saloons 27 and 29. Dating from 1892 and built by G F Milnes they are probably the most elegant of the horse car fleet and at one time were referred to as the Pullmans.

The tramway has four winter saloons in its fleet for use on very wet days. Here the third of a batch of three, No.29 stands outside the depot on a grey July day in 2005. Just possibly it will rain and the tram will find itself pressed into service later in the day.

The casual visitor to the tramway would rightly assume that car No.1 is the oldest in the fleet but, it is actually the newest car still in operation today. Cars 48 - 50 were built several years after this car was completed in 1913 at a cost of £252 3s 6d. The original No.1 was a double deck car delivered for the opening of the tramway in 1876, it had disappeared by 1901.

Below: A view inside the workshop area shows car 42 awaiting attention along with a good collection of cycles. This open toastrack car was delivered in 1905 at a grand cost of £63!

Below: A general view of the inside of the depot with preserved Upper Douglas Cable Car No.72/73 to the right of the picture. Other cars visible are 27, 18 and nearest the camera on the left 29.

Two other surviving cars that resided until recently at Homefield are Vulcan No.49 and covered toastrack No.47. It is also hoped that these two cars will one day return to the tramway and maybe see passenger service again.

Below: Another view inside the workshop area, this time of sister cars 43 and 44 of 1907. Car 44 is known as the Royal car after having been used by members of the Royal family on more that one occasion. Car 43 is undergoing a complete repaint in this view taken on 9th September 2008.

Below: The oldest horse car that survives is No.11. This tram has not seen service for many years and was until recently stored in the former Isle of Man Road Services Homefield bus depot, in upper Douglas. Maybe one day it will be returned to active service.

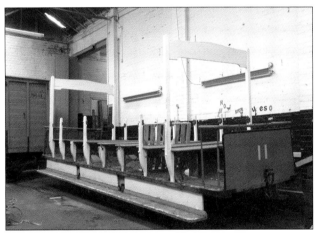

The upper deck of car 18 provided the vantage point for this view of cars 29 and 1 resting between duties inside the depot. The tram on the left of the picture is 21 and that just visible on the right is 35.

Derby Castle caused nearly half a day,s service to be cancelled on the 31st August 2002. Services eventually got underway around 13.00.

The 2003 season was shortened as the growing costs of the tramway threatened its future, the tramway only operating from the beginning of May to the end of September. The tramway was promoted with a number of banners being placed at prominent roadside locations around the town at the start of the 2004 season. The Lieutenant Governor and his family visited the horse stables during the year to see the horse Mark, adopted by his family during the 2001 adopt a horse scheme.

Douglas Corporation looked at the idea of running some illuminated cars for the run up to Christmas 2004 but sadly the idea never got off the ground. The tramway was closed along with a large part of the Promenade to accommodate the security required around the Villa Marina for the British Irish Conference on the 20th May 2005.

In an attempt to reduce the number of cars left parked across the tracks and outside the depot at Derby Castle, barriers and large no parking signage were put in place.

Only 76,478 passengers travelled on the tramway in 2005, the trams covering around 20,000 miles. This represents a drop of over 100,000 on the 1995 figure with the mileage covered being less than a third of that of 1995.

Despite some cosmetic attention in April and the car moving into the tram depot in May, car No.11 was moved to Homefield on the 21st September 2005 for undercover storage, as no time had been available for its full restoration and return to service.

The local fire service had requested the suspension of tramway services along the Promenade during the race periods, to reduce traffic congestion. Thankfully the Corporation rejected the request.

After the success of the local Commonwealth Games team in Australia, Douglas Corporation provided double-deck horse tram No.18 to convey the athletes and officials along the Promenade from the Sea Terminal to the Villa Marina for a reception on the 20th April 2006.

Fares for the 2006 season were reduced to £1.00 single and the all day tickets were withdrawn, a move intended to encourage more to use the tramway.

It was suggested that a spare Horse Tramway car should be put on static display on the short length of cable tramway track laid at the bottom of Victoria Street but potential damage to the car by late night revellers resulted in the idea being shelved.

A further threat to the future of the Horse Tramway came when the Corporation announced that it needed to cut overall expenses by £180,000. However, the tramway survived the cuts and the 2007 season produced little change to the service, although car 36 did return to traffic after a number of years absent.

However, since the end of the 2007 season, the tramway has been the subject of much discussion. The hidden cost of clearing up after the horses was raised at a Corporation meeting and the possibility of the horses wearing nappies was considered!

In January 2008 it was announced that the tramway had lost £270,000 the previous year and that the 2008 season would be shortened by four weeks, starting in mid May and finishing in mid September. The service frequency would also be reduced and the possibility of not having conductors was considered, as was running non-stop along the Promenades. The only change implemented was the reduction in the operating season. At the December meeting of the Borough Council, members were told that the operating deficit for the 2008 season had been reduced by £20,000 despite a further reduction in passenger numbers.

At the same meeting came the news that for the 2009 season the trams would start later in the morning at 11.00 and continue into the evening, finishing at 20.00. The Council Leader gave his backing to keeping the trams, at that meeting adding that the lack of the Summerland complex or a replacement attraction was a factor in the passenger reductions.

The double deck tram was out in service every day, occasionally more than once and generally the season went well. The biggest break from the normal came towards the end of the year with the announcement that Santa trams would run in the week running up to Christmas.

The tramway staff decorated tram No.1 with lights inside and out and provided some appropriate horse names. The operation was a resounding success with all trams booked up in advance and the weather obliged with sunshine on all three days. Soon after the operation, the idea of corporate charters was being considered. The future of this tramway is far from certain but; initiatives such as these must be seen as positive. The tramway is a vital part of the transport heritage of the Island and any efforts to secure its future are welcomed.

Many visitors to the Island enquire about the welfare of the motive power, the horses. The truth is that they are extremely well looked after, spending the winter months grazing in fields around the Island specially reserved for them. During the operating season they are stabled near the Derby Castle terminus and only work three return trips each, in any one day. Indeed, it is claimed that they can count and then stop automatically at the stables at the end of their stint!

THE MANX ELECTRIC RAILWAY

The first plans for a railway from Douglas to Laxey and Ramsey came in 1882 with the formation of the Douglas, Laxey & Ramsey Railway Co., with a line leaving the steam railway at Quarterbridge, climbing towards Onchan and on to Laxey. This proposal came to nothing, as did a number of other projects, including an adventurous plan to tunnel through Bank Hill with a line starting near the steam railway terminus in Douglas.

However, in 1892, Alexander Bruce, Manager of Dumbells Bank in Douglas since 1878, and Frederick Saunderson, an engineer who had come from Ireland in 1865 and who had connections with the family of Richard Rowe, Captain of the Laxey Mines, sought and were granted powers by Tynwald to develop Howstrake estate, an area to the north of Douglas. The estate was purchased in the name of Mr Saunderson, with backing from a Mr Alfred Lusty, a wealthy London merchant who had retired to the Island and lived at Howstrake. Douglas Bay Estates Ltd was registered in September 1892 with a capital of £50,000, construction of an electric tramway getting under way as soon as possible, the first stage of what is now known as the Manx Electric Railway.

Electrification was carried out by Mather & Platt of Salford Ironworks, while G.F. Milnes of Birkenhead built the first three tramcars along with six trailers. The area now occupied by the depot at Derby Castle was once an inlet of the sea and was filled in to carry the tramway past, the area behind being big enough to accommodate the depot and

Derby Castle station area has changed many times through the life of the Manx Electric Railway. In recent years the waiting room provided has been a Horse Tram, Leyland National Bus, Former Lisbon Tramcar and is now this bus style shelter complete with Manx Electric Titling. Two pairs of trams are preparing for the first departures of the day and below the Electric Railway sign in the hillside in the distance can be seen the depot top shed, a view not possible until the recent demolition of the Summerland complex.

On 7th September 1993 the Manx Electric celebrated its centenary. Following the formalities of a ceremony at Derby Castle, trams 1 and 2 took invited guests to Groudle for a reception in the Groudle public house and the unveiling of a centenary plaque at Groudle. Here we see a sparkling car No.1 at Derby Castle with special headboard prior to departure for Groudle. Car 7 looks on.

Manx Electric cars 1 and 2 represent the two oldest tramcars in the world still operating on their original line. The two see little use in service but are often called upon to operate specials on the line. On one such occasion car No.2 was preparing for departure from Derby Castle on 21st July 2008 with a special to Laxey. As can be seen from this picture they are kept in immaculate condition.

power station. The name Derby Castle was that of a private dwelling which was taken over to allow construction of a ballroom and theatre complex.

The line officially opened on the 7th September 1893, carrying 20,000 passengers between then and the 28th September when services were suspended to allow construction to begin of an extension to Laxey, approved by Tynwald on the 17th November 1893. The line was doubled throughout its length, the Groudle Viaduct built and a terminus near the present depot at Laxey constructed, opening on the 27th July 1894. To accommodate the increase in traffic expected with the extension to Laxey, six more tramcars were delivered from G.F. Milnes during 1894,

after completion at a cost of around £40,000, the line was sold to the Isle of Man Tramways & Electric Power Co. Ltd for £72,500!

The success of the Douglas to Laxey line prompted the company to petition Tynwald for a further extension to Ramsey. Although consent was not received until the 1st November 1897, it seems likely that some land preparation had already started. Ballure was reached by July 1898 and Ramsey by July 1899, bringing the total length of the line to

The rebuilt Snaefell car No.7 is seen here in its new guise as Manx Electric works car No.34. Located between the two cabs is a generator enabling the locomotive to operate over the line while the overhead power is isolated.

On a dull July day in 2008, car 19 has its overhead pole repositioned during shunting operations. Each time the car changes direction it is necessary to turn the pole to trail the direction of travel. Once in contact with the overhead wire the pole allows the tram to collect 500 volts DC, this providing all the power the tram needs in service.

along with six more trailers, all bearing the name Douglas & Laxey Coast Electric Tramway Co. Ltd on their bodysides, the name to which the company had changed during the construction of the Laxey extension. The company name was changed again, to Isle of Man Tramways & Electric Power Co., when the Douglas Horse Tramway was purchased on the 30th April 1894. Control of the horse tramway was taken from the 1st May. Part of the deal of purchasing the horse tramway was the requirement to construct a cable tramway to serve the Upper Douglas area and the Upper Douglas Cable Tramway, as it was known, opened on the 15th August 1896.

Construction of the Snaefell Mountain Railway from Laxey to near the summit of the Island's highest mountain was undertaken in 1895. It opened on the 21st August and,

17 miles (28.5 km). The official opening ceremony of the extension was held on the 24th July 1899.

Dumbells Bank collapsed in February 1900, with outstanding loans to the Railway of £150,000, causing the Isle of Man Tramways & Electric Power Co., and a considerable number of other companies, to go into receivership. A £225,000 offer from the British Electric Traction Co. for the entire undertaking was rejected in 1901. Douglas Corporation offered £50,000 for the horse tramway and cable tramway in late 1901 and this was duly accepted. January 1902 saw an offer accepted from a Manchester-based syndicate, backed by a continental merchant banker, for £250,000 for the electric tramway, the final settlement being made in September 1902.

The Manx Electric Railway Company was incorporated in London in November 1902 and proceeded to purchase the tramway from the Manchester syndicate for £370,000. The financial problems of this period were compounded by the involvement of several senior members of the Isle of Man Tramways & Electric Power Co. in the Blackpool & Fleetwood Tramway Co. Ltd, that had built the eight-mile long system there to the mainland standard gauge of 4' 8½" with much of the rolling stock of similar design to that on the Island.

The new company had considerable problems in its early days, with unreliable equipment and a backlog of maintenance. Much re-equipping took place both to the rolling stock and to the permanent way, and by 1906 the line was as up to date as any other.

The Manx Electric soon became a valuable asset for the Island's residents, as well as being a visitor attraction with its

During the mid 1990's several major railway events were held, one feature of which were evening photography sessions. On one such occasion several photographers had persuaded a motorman to position car No.2 adjacent to the Summerland building to create an unusual nocturnal picture. Needless to say in the true spirit of the Isle of Man Railways, the staff obliged with a smile.

increasingly old rolling stock and beautiful scenery. However, during the period between 1928 and 1932, a serious accident and three setbacks befell the line.

On the 8th August 1928 car No.1 with trailer No. 39 well laden, had stopped in the Fairy Cottage area to collect overhead maintenance staff, when car No.16 with trailer No.56, also well laden, came round the curve and was unable to stop, causing a serious rear end collision resulting in 32 people being injured. An enquiry resulted in the stopping on curves being banned.

The greatest loss to the system occurred on the night of the 5th April 1930 when fire broke out in the Laxey car shed, destroying motor cars Nos.3, 4, 8 and 24, seven trailer cars, all three tower wagons, a mail van and much other equipment. Only the depot and three trailers were rebuilt. Later in 1930, serious flooding in Laxey after a violent storm

was blamed on the Manx Electric's weir which formed part of the company's generating station. A court ruling ordered the company to clear 4-5,000 tons of rubbish from the river bed and pay all the legal costs.

The third disaster occurred on the 3rd April 1932, when fire destroyed the hotel and refreshment room at Dhoon Glen, which were never rebuilt.

The Second World War brought unexpected prosperity to the Island, which was used extensively for prisoners of war.

High on the wall of the workshops in the depot at Derby Castle is this plaque commemorating the opening of the line through to Laxey on 28th July 1894.

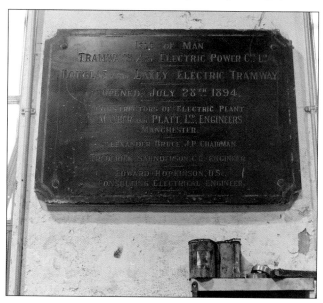

The Manx Electric survived this period of uncertainty and in 1945 was used to film a scene for 'I See a Dark Stranger'.

The immediate post-war period saw the Manx Electric enjoying the benefits of increasing tourism but in the early fifties a decline in numbers of visitors and passengers led the company to tell Tynwald that it would be unable to continue trading after the 30th September 1956. The entire system was offered for sale for £70,000.

Tynwald, not wanting to lose the Manx Electric as it was still an important tourist attraction and local lifeline, commissioned a report by a team from British Railways. This was soon rejected and a second report, by an independent team, led to the nationalisation of the system on the 6th November 1956. The Manx Electric Railway Act was signed on the 17th April 1957, creating the Manx Electric Railway Board of Tynwald.

For the next few years money was forthcoming for maintenance and investment in new track and equipment, 200 tons of rail and 3,000 sleepers being delivered. A start

During a one day visit to the Island in February 1995 the Author visited the depot and took this picture of Manx Electric saloon trailer No.57, an unidentified Snaefell Mountain car and illuminated car No.9, decorated for the forthcoming 'International Railway Festival' all receiving attention.

Standing in the workshop area of the new top shed at Derby Castle is re-built winter saloon No.22 in the company if sister cars 19 and 21. The working conditions within the new shed are considerably improved on what was available before.

Current health and safety regulations have brought about the creation of this overhead wire maintenance vehicle. Built on the chassis of former trailer car No.52 the hydraulic platform with its sturdy wooded surrounds make working on the overhead simple and safe. Here the vehicle has the finishing touches applied to a new paint job during November 2008.

In February 1995 construction of the disabled trailer was under way. This picture shows the modifications to the frame of the tram prior to receiving the new bodywork. The widened frames are clearly visible.

was made on repainting the tramcars in a standard livery of green and cream but the objections to this were so severe that it was soon abandoned. The Derby Castle to Laxey section was relaid completely during this period, while the Laxey to Ramsey section was found to be in very good order. This period of relative buoyancy was followed by leaner times when only essential work was carried out.

On the 20th January 1967 part of the retaining wall at Bulgham slipped away followed on the 28th January by a further slip causing a section of trackbed to fall into the sea. This gave the Government a chance to show its commitment to the line. Perhaps surprisingly, crossovers were installed at either side of the breach and passengers transferred from one car to another on foot. Contractors were called in and on the 10th July through services were resumed.

The early 1970s saw a privatisation bid from Rapid Transit Technical Services. With the line in serious danger of closure, they proposed a complete revision of services, a new workshop at Laxey serving the Snaefell Railway as well, new power supplies and marketing initiatives. Nothing came of this offer and, within a short time, Transmark (a division of British Rail) had been called in to report on the future of the line. Their broad conclusion was that the line would cease to make a loss only if it was closed down. Part, and thankfully only part, of this recommendation was carried out, the

Laxey to Ramsey section closing on the 30th September 1975 despite considerable public protest.

Interestingly the following year there was a general election on the Island and, with transport being a major issue, many of the 'anti' members were not re-elected. The new Government soon reacted to public pressure and the Laxey to Ramsey line reopened on the 25th June 1977, enjoying a buoyant season.

In early 1977 the Manx Electric Railway Board took over the running of the steam railway, the two lines doing reasonably well despite falling visitor numbers. In April 1980 the Board took over the bus services as well and it was reformed as the Isle of Man Passenger Transport Board in 1983. It became part of the Department of Tourism and Transport in 1986.

On the 1st December 1987 Mr Robert Smith was appointed Transport Executive, having previously worked for London Transport. Many of the cars received major overhaul over the next few years, a programme that is ongoing. Disaster returned to the line on the night of the 30th September 1990 when car No.22 caught fire in Derby Castle depot and was completely destroyed but, once again, Government commitment was shown and a new No. 22 was built on the original chassis, re-entering service in May 1992.

In preparation for the 1993 celebrations the former

Ramsey goods shed was converted into a small museum about the Manx Electric Railway and Snaefell Mountain Railway. Trailer No. 59 represented the tram fleet, the rest of the area featuring display boards and a cab mock-up of an Snaefell car.

The year 1993 was designated the 'Year of Railways' to celebrate the centenary of the line. The festivities were officially launched at Derby Castle on Saturday the 10th April 1993 by Lieutenant Governor Air Marshal Sir Laurence Jones who drove car No.1 through a celebration banner. Car 9 was chosen to become the Island's first illuminated tram. It was inaugurated later the same day and was, and still is, often used on the evening services to Groudle.

Loco No.23, with bogies borrowed from car No.17, made a test run on the line on the 9th June 1993 and later in the year took part in the celebrations. Car 26 was used extensively during the season for Motorman lessons for members of the public.

Steam Railway locomotive No.4 arrived by road and operated a number of steam trips between Laxey and Dhoon Quarry hauling closed trailers Nos.57 and 58.

Centenary day, Tuesday the 7th September 1993, began with a formal gathering at Derby Castle with invited guests being addressed by the Lieutenant Governor and Minister for Tourism Alan Bell MHK. Following the formal bit, the Lieutenant Governor drove car No.1 hauling trailer 13 to Groudle for a reception in the Groudle Hotel and the unveiling of a centenary plaque at the Laxey end of the station.

Unusually, Santa trams operated on the line in connection with the Santa events on the Groudle Glen Railway.

The longest stretch of track relay for many years took place over the 1993/94 winter, from Ballagorry to Dolland, while the section from Howstrake to Groudle had its overhead refurbished.

Trailer 56 was moved to Derby Castle in 1994 for conversion to a wheelchair accessible trailer, to allow wheelchair passengers to enjoy a trip on the line. For a short while during the season car Nos.2 and 6 assumed the identity of sister cars 3 and 8, both of which had been lost in the Laxey fire.

The year 1995 marked the centenary of the Snaefell Mountain Railway and an 'International Railway Festival' was held. A grand cavalcade took place through Laxey station on Sunday the 20th August as part of the celebrations, with virtually all serviceable Manx Electric cars and many sundry items taking part.

During the winter of 1995/96 the crossings at Halfway and Laxey No.3, Princess Motors were relaid. The winter service only operated between Laxey and Ramsey to accommodate these works.

Towards the end of 1995 plans were announced for the replacement of the Derby Castle top shed, the one parallel with the running lines. The £600,000 project would replace the original shed that was in a poor state of repair and, by default, used to house the vast majority of the priceless rolling stock.

Former Lisbon tram No.360 arrived on the Manx Electric on the 3rd June 1996. The tram arrived at Ramsey on board the Mezeron Freight Group vessel the Silver River and was transported to Douglas by road.

Car No.9 had her illuminated panels changed to promote the Groudle Glen Railway centenary. During the railway events built around the Groudle celebrations, a couple of cars were once again renumbered to take up the guise of sister vehicles destroyed in the Laxey fire; Nos.4 and 24 were played by 6 and 26.

A new generator was acquired to allow Manx Electric cars to operate on the steam railway or on their own line in the absence of power. It was mounted on wagon No.8.

The old top shed was emptied during September and October, locomotive No.23 being the first to leave on the 25th September. Some of the stock went to the steam railway for storage while a long line of trams stretched along the southbound line from Laxey car sheds across the viaduct and nearly into the station. These were covered with tarpaulins.

The 1996/97 winter service only operated between Laxey and Ramsey for the second year running, this partly due to the rebuilding at Derby Castle sheds and associated works at the depot entrance.

A policy decision to keep cars 1 and 2 in different sheds was taken during the 1997 season to prevent the loss of both in a disaster, while a shortage of available trams led to some passengers being turned away at Derby Castle. This shortage was due to a couple of trams still being stored on the steam railway, following the rebuilding and on-going problems with the new Derby Castle top shed.

Over the winter of 1997/98 maintenance work included renewal of a number of the overhead poles between Derby Castle and Groudle. The winter storms caused some problems at Garwick and Laxey.

The need to turn off the overhead power supply for a day on the 24th October 1997 resulted in what must rate as the most unusual passenger train to have operated on the line. Car 21 was coupled to wagon 8 with the generator and operated as a diesel electric between Derby Castle and Laxey

In the depths of the top shed, motor cars 33 and 7 undergo varying levels of overhaul. Car 7 is in for a major rebuild after being pressed into engineering duties as part of the massive relaying programme and consequential outside storage.

The rebuilt trailer 56 nearing completion in the Derby Castle works. The original ends of the trailer have been retained, with just the centre section widened to allow full wheelchair access.

A splendid line up of winter saloons during an evening photo session. At today's ages this picture represents a combined tram age of 330 years. Despite their age these cars still provide the backbone of the services to the northern end of the line in Ramsey.

A daytime line up has cars 1 and 2 together along with 26 and 5. The latter two are standing within the old top shed, an entirely wooden structure, replaced in the late 1990's by the new modern shed.

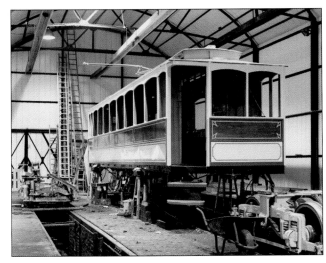

Car No.19 undergoing bogie overhaul and repaint in the workshop area of the lower sheds at derby Castle. In recent years these sheds has been brightened up by re-painting, re-cladding and new lighting.

Lisbon car No.360 poses outside the bottom shed at Derby castle. Sadly this is about as far as the car ever got, indeed the Authors only journey in the car under its own power was along this shed road and back!

A daytime view of the same car in just about the same place. It is interesting to compare the 1893 wooden bodied Manx Electric car No.1 with this 1907 fully enclosed car. It was purchased by the Manx Electric in 1996.

The view from Imperial Terrace of car No.21 approaching Port Jack with a through service from Ramsey during June 2006. The modern building up to the left of the tram is Skandia House, built to replace the old Douglas Bay Hotel building.

In an attempt to promote an intigrated transport system, car No.22 was painted into a livery similar to the bus fleet for a couple of years. The car looked somewhat different although arguably smart in these colours. It is seen approaching Port Jack with a southbound service. (Miles Cowsill)

for the day.

Meanwhile car 33 that was in store on the steam railway made a similar rare working on the 2nd December when, with wagon and generator, it made a return trip to Port Erin. The trip was repeated the following day, this time with a dozen or so invited railway press on board, to promote the forthcoming Steam 125 celebrations of 1998. The tram was driven on the two days by Cathie Antrobus of Isle of Man Transport.

Plans were being drawn up to put locomotive No.23 into operational condition for 1999, which was the centenary of the completion of the line through to Ramsey. It was also proposed that 23 should form the centrepiece at the 2000 Warley National Model Railway Exhibition at the NEC in Birmingham. Sadly this did not materialize. Car 33 returned to the MER for Ramsey Sprint day, traditionally the busiest day of the year for the line. A new road crossing was installed at Howstrake to allow construction access to a new housing estate at Groudle.

Floods returned on the 24th October 1998 when, after a severe storm, Laxey station was flooded and Cornaa was also affected. The storm caused severe damage on the mountain road resulting in its closure and plans to relay the Ballure crossing on the outskirts of Ramsey over the coming winter

were postponed due to the increased traffic using the coastal road.

Santa trams once again operated in conjunction with the Groudle Santa weekend.

Much of 1999 was dominated by the continuing problems with the new top shed at Derby Castle, the entire track layout having been relaid at least once already.

The year 1999 was the centenary of the line reaching the current Ramsey station and the Manx Electric as we know it today. A number of events were staged in and around Ramsey station to mark the anniversary.

In August 1999 a planning application was made to refurbish the Laxey car shed, with doors at the Laxey end only, effectively reducing the shed from four tracks to three.

In an encouraging move the winter service for 1999/2000 was augmented with the addition of weekend services, the first Saturday winter services since 1975, the first Sunday's for considerably longer. Fares were halved to levels in line with the bus service and tickets were interchangeable between the two. The road crossing at Ballabeg was relaid over the winter, single line operation being maintained throughout.

To mark the beginning of the new millennium and the Manx Electric Railway passing into its third century, a special

After climbing past Skandia House and Onchan Head station, the line levels off and runs along beside King Edward Road before climbing again towards Howstrake. Here Toastrack power car No.26 heads a special charter past the backs of the houses of King Edward Park.

tram operated on Wednesday the 5th January 2000. Car No.1 departed from Derby Castle at 09.00 for Groudle, the first tram of the new century. It returned to Derby Castle as the 09.20 service car. On arrival at Derby Castle it was swapped with car 20 for the rest of the day's operation.

A new café opened inside the station building at Laxey and in an arrangement with the Department of Agriculture, Fisheries & Forestry, the Dhoon Glen station café also reopened. The former Lisbon tram became the waiting room at Derby Castle on the 4th May 2000, replacing Leyland National Bus 26.

Car 5 emerged from Derby Castle towards the end of the 2000 season with its titling in Manx.

The 2000/01 winter service was four return trips each way Monday to Saturday and three on Sunday. A full colour winter timetable was produced that also gave details of the forthcoming summer service dates.

In January 2001 a number of items from Laxey car shed were moved to Derby Castle and then by road to the former Homefield bus depot, following the move of the bus operation to the new facility at Banks Circus adjacent to the steam railway workshops.

Derby Castle yard was relaid again in February 2001 in an effort to further improve the situation there, while an announcement from Government brought good news. The sum of £600,000 had been made available to fund track

relaying over the coming winter, with a further £12m over the next nine years.

There was rumour that the Laxey substation equipment including the fascinating mercury arc rectifiers would be replaced but this has come to nothing. Thought was also being given to converting a ratchet car to a diesel electric works car but nothing has ever come of this either.

The plans to refurbish Laxey car shed had lapsed and were replaced with more ambitious plans to demolish the existing shed, itself a replacement in 1931, and replace it with a new structure.

A further £1.1million worth of track relaying was carried out over the 2001/02 winter and a number of overhead poles repainted. New tramstop signs were erected along the line to the same style as the bus stops but with a tram instead of bus design. Port-e-Vullen received a new shelter following the demolition of the original decayed structure.

The Manx Electric Railway Society, concerned about the future fate of some rolling stock and buildings, agreed a conservation policy with the then Minister of Tourism and Leisure.

The winter service with four return trips operated through the 2001/02 and 2002/03 winters, with colour timetable leaflets being produced.

Car 21 appeared in service with Isle of Man Transport stickers below the cab windows on each end. The body of

1893 built car No.2 passing the outskirts of Onchan with the first tram of the day to Laxey. The line runs alongside King Edward Road as far as Halfway, a point near the Liverpool Arms hotel.

Another view of car No.26 having left the outskirts of Onchan behind and beginning the climb to Howstrake. The pair are approaching a crossover and Howstrake Golf course is up to the right of the tram.

Re-build winter saloon No.22 with an unidentified trailer is seen approaching Howstrake station. In a few yards the passengers will loose the view of Douglas Bay completely. In the distance can be seen the Carnane transmitter station.

Viewed from the boundary of Howstrake Golf course, winter saloon No.19 is captured while working towards Derby Castle with a late afternoon service from Ramsey on 21st September 2008. Howstrake station building can be seen in the distance.

Lisbon car 360 was removed from its home at Derby Castle station on the 19th April and replaced by an elongated bus-style shelter repositioned across the end of the tracks, the new shelter becoming operational in June 2002.

Flood damage returned to the line once again on the night of the 21st October 2002, when a severe storm affected much of the Island. The engineers shed at Derby Castle was damaged from the cliff behind and the ballast was washed away in a couple of places, with debris being dumped across the track in several places by the excess water. It took until Friday the 25th to get the line open throughout and that was with some single line working.

Several new shelters were provided between Onchan Head and Howstrake and the Laxey car shed stop received a tarmac base although no building.

The massive relay programme continued through the 2002/03 winter, while in a break with tradition, three trams

Car Nos 1 and 2 at Groudle after arrival with the centenary specials from Derby Castle on 7th September 1993. The Power cars and trailers have been shunted and are ready for the return trip. The archways in the distance lead to a private residence on the upper slopes of Groudle Glen.

were repainted at Ramsey car shed by local contractor Brian O'Hare.

The Derby Castle booking office received a repaint during April 2003. The depot wall was enhanced with a series of paintings by London Artist Cian Quayle. Ballagawne received a new shelter while Dhoon Quarry finally lost its shelter, Ballajora was repaired and painted during May/June 2003. Cornaa shelter had a complete new front and repaint.

The Laxey car shed saga continued with the removal of the roof of the shed for safety reasons, at the same time as the former Ramsey goods shed was converted into a youth centre. Named 'The Shed' the new facility was officially

opened on the 16th November 2003.

The 2003/04 winter service was operated with just two return trips daily and although standing passengers were carried on the first day, the numbers soon trailed off. Considerable relaying was due over the 2003/04 winter although there was no work planned for the following winter. Laxey goods shed was used to store overhead wire equipment. A further batch of trams, Nos.1, 2, 33 and trailer 61 were repainted over the winter at Ramsey.

The evening services, except the Groudle trips, were not included in the 2004 summer timetable. The following winter service announcement was delayed as plans to demolish the Summerland complex were being discussed.

The former Laxey station café was demolished amidst

Tunnel car No.6 with a winter saloon trailer in tow trundles past Groudle while working a service from Laxey. No.6 is one of six cars built for the opening of the extension from Groudle to Laxey in 1894. The Groudle public house is visible behind the tram.

much protest during the summer of 2004 after being declared unsafe.

Storms returned to the Island and the Manx Electric on the night of the 7/8th January 2005, with winds in excess of 100mph being recorded in a number of places. The overhead was brought down in several places, in most cases by falling trees and piles of debris from the trees and buildings blocked the line. The line closed as a result with the winter service suspended and reopened just in time for the summer season on the 21st March.

Fares for the 2005 season were held at 2004 levels while the use of Island 12-trip bus tickets previously accepted on the railways was suspended.

The Dhoon Glen café was closed for the first part of the 2005 season while a new tenant was found and Ballabeg, Cornaa and Dreemskerry station buildings were refurbished

During the early evening of 9th August 2006, illuminated car No.9 and trailer 42 pass Groudle with a service to Laxey. The road is still with the tramway and the large Groudle station building is visible behind the tram.

Approaching the junction with Bibaloe Beg is winter saloon No.22 with trailer 41 in tow. The pair are working a through service from Derby Castle to Ramsey on 4th July 2008. The warm weather has tempted many passengers to ride in the relative open of the trailer.

During the late 1950's a start was made on repainting the fleet into a new standard livery of green and cream Objections were fierce and the idea was soon dropped. However, in order to have a reminder of those times operational on the line today, open toastrack No.16 and trailer 60 were repainted into the historic livery and prove popular with enthusiasts when used in service. On this occasion working a special, the pair are seen approaching Halfway on 21st July 2008.

The crossing at Halfway is in common with others on the line, only protected by lights and no barriers are installed. With the road lights flashing red, 1893 built car No.2 crosses with an additional service from Laxey to Derby Castle on 21st July 2008.

During 1994 and early 1995, trailer car 56 was converted into a disabled saloon from its original covered toastrack type. Car 22 with the trailer is captured on an outing to convey a wheelchair-bound passenger from Laxey to Derby Castle. The pair are captured crossing the main Douglas to Ramsey road at Halfway.

Having left Garwick the line re-emerges from the trees and again runs alongside the main road for a short while. Rounding the sharp curve Car No.22 is about to cross the C26 road that casually points to Creg-ny-Baa, an interesting destination as that road does not actually go there!

Beyond Baldrine there are a number of sharp curves as the line weaves its way through housing. Approaching Baldrine station and crossing Baldrine Road, with a service from Ramsey is car No.22 with trailer 40 on 12th July 2008.

Garwick Glen used to be a bustling station with many passengers alighting to visit the Glen below. Nowadays it is rare to even stop and so no opportunity is missed by enthusiast organised specials to stop and take a picture or two. Here with one such special is car No.26 and trailer 47, pausing for those pictures, while the driver discusses the driving controls with the Authors wife.

Open toastrack and trailer, Nos 16 and 60 crossing the Main A2 road at Ballabeg, while operating a special from Derby castle to Ramsey during July 2008.

Shortly after crossing the road is the station at Ballabeg. Although few trams actually stop, local residents have taken the station under their wing and provide a splendid display of bedding plants, keep the building and other structures painted and clean. Here car No.26 pauses for a photo stop while working a special to Ramsey.

The next station is Fairy Cottage, not to be confused with the Fairy Bridge, where we see winter saloon No.19 operating a late season service towards Derby Castle.

The Fairy Cottage station building is just visible to the left of the picture, the houses of Pinfold Hill are on the right, Car No.21 passes with a winter service to Ramsey.

On 15th April 1930 fire destroyed the original Laxey car shed and a number of power and trailer cars. The 1930's replacement shed seen here has now been demolished in preparation for the construction of a modern shed.

Below: During the last decade or so, Laxey car shed has seen little use, it being used mainly for the storage of spare rolling stock. However, on some occasions it has been used for the storage of steam locomotives and rare combinations. Here we see ratchet car No.18 with disabled trailer 56 outside the shed in 1995.

Below: A view inside the shed with illuminated car No.9 centre stage, car No.22 on the right and some stored trailers and a van on the left. The stored rolling stock was later moved to Homefield, the former Isle of Man Road services bus depot in upper Douglas.

Below: The new car shed was completed during the early part of 2009, the trackwork a few months later. This view shows the completed shed before it was connected to the main line.

Below: Two wiring trolleys keep company with a variety of power and trailer cars inside Laxey car shed. The style wiring trolleys have recently given way to the type illustrated earlier in the book. The uneven floor of the old shed is clearly evident in this view.

With the roof removed the poor state of the old shed becomes evident. An old wiring trolley, trailer 62, power car 32, a new wiring trolley and a simplex keep each other company inside the shed. Photographed in July 2008.

Shortly after passing the car shed the line crosses Rencell Hill and then the Laxey Sub Station. This wonderful marble switch panel, with its collection of copper bladed switches and polished black amp meters is a superb reminder of early electrical installations.

Below: As with any railway the Manx Electric has a number of works vehicles. On loan to the overhead wire gang is open power car No.27, complete with makeshift windscreen to protect the driver from some of the winter weather. It has with it two of the older style wiring trolleys. The crew discuss the day's work before returning the ensemble to Laxey Car sheds.

Below; On a quieter day in April 2007, car No.19 arrives with a trailer on a service from Ramsey. The Mines Tavern is to the right of the picture the mountains above the village of Agneash are in the distance.

During busy periods, in particular on good days, a good number of passengers travel to Laxey and then transfer to the Snaefell line. This often requires extra cars to operate just as far as Laxey. The siding alongside the former goods shed is used to park these cars before they return to Derby Castle. Car No.2 has completed its running round and has shunted back into the siding to await its call to return south.

Below: Scenes such as this were commonplace when the author first visited the Island in the mid 1970's but sadly are now a rare occurrence. On 20th August 2006 a ceremony was held in the Glen gardens to re-start the second Laxey Wheel after its rescue from Cornwall and full restoration. At the end of the afternoon the Manx Electric carried huge numbers back to Derby Castle and indeed to Ramsey. Car No.20 and Trailer 48 will soon be full but, in true MER tradition, the next car will be just a few minutes behind.

On the 18th July 2008, a small celebration was held in Laxey station to mark the re-opening of the Laxey to Ramsey section of the line. It had been announced that the section would remain closed for the whole season due to unsafe trackwork but, outcry in Tynwald and the intervention of the Chief Minister allowed a few weeks of through running on a single track. (John Davis)

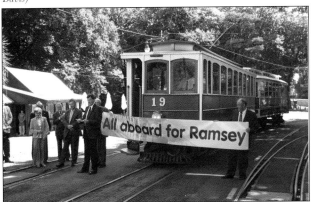

As part of the 1993 'Year of Railways' a cavalcade was run at Laxey with just about every moveable piece of rolling stock taking place. Here fully restored locomotive No.23 is seen with wagon No.21 in tow. The wagon dates from 1895 and started life as a passenger power car similar in appearance to the Snaefell fleet. The pair are seen approaching the station area while taking part in the cavalcade.

A fine study of illuminated car No.9 pausing between duties alongside the former goods shed at Laxey. Plans are in hand to turn this building into a Manx Electric Heritage centre. Photographed in May 2006.

Shortly after leaving the station the line crosses the main road through the village and then almost immediately, Mines Road that leads up to the famous Laxey Wheel. Car 21 with trailer are crossing Mines Road on a working to Ramsey. Car 21 is in a short lived livery incorporating the Isle of Man Transport logo on the ends.

The top of Captains Hill affords this view of Manx Electric cars arriving in Laxey from Ramsey, with the Laxey Mines Railway nestling below. Car No.22 with an empty trailer 44 pass one of the Mines Railway locomotives letting off steam.

Leaving Laxey the line climbs up the north side of the valley before turning and heading for the highest point on the route at Bulgham. In the area of Skincoes Farm car No.21 is running wrong line towards Laxey. This was the result of safety concerns and the near curtailment of all services between Laxey and Ramsey during 2008. Following some emergency funding enough re-laying was completed to open one track linking the two towns. 7th September 2008.

and repainted.

The demolition of the Summerland complex was finally to go ahead over the winter of 2005/06. This would require the track to be lifted from the Derby Castle depot entrance down to the station and hence there would be no access for the trams and the winter service was cancelled. The opportunity was taken to relay a further 1.25 miles of track over the same winter. The overhead at Port Jack was refurbished and a number of new poles installed.

A Ruston Hornsby diesel shunter was used to assist the relaying during the winter. Named Bertie, the loco dates from 1949. Meanwhile a new retractable wiring wagon was constructed using the chassis of original wagon No.8.

The Summerland demolition went ahead as planned, the Department of Transport taking advantage of the closed railway to relay the crossing just to the north of Laxey station that takes the three tracks, two Manx Electric and one Snaefell, across the main road through the village. The

The rugged terrain of this area is evident from this view of Car No.22 nearing the end of the climb up from Laxey, while working a through service to Ramsey. Soon the pair will turn sharp left and being the run down to Dhoon Glen station.

finished product greatly enhances the whole area with footpaths for pedestrians crossing into Ham and Egg Terrace incorporated. There was no further news regarding the proposed development of Laxey car sheds.

The Director of Public Transport resigned from his post in February, returning to his Sussex home.

The demolition of the Summerland complex delayed the start of the 2006 operating season, the first trams running on the 15th May. The relay between the depot entrance and Derby Castle station could not be started until the demolition was almost complete. Local residents tidied up the Ballabeg

station area, provided planters and plenty of summer bedding plants to give an enhanced look.

The overall state and the outside storage of car No.7 in the roofless Laxey car shed, was the subject of a Tynwald debate on the 21st March 2006.

The winter 2006/07 service only operated at weekends and the Baldrine and Groudle road crossings were both relaid. The Isle of Man Transport branding was dropped in early 2007 and the railways returned to their previous identity as Isle of Man Railways. The winter service drew to a close on the 1st April 2007 and with it possibly the end of winter services on the line, certainly for the foreseeable future.

The issue of car No.7 was raised in Tynwald again, with the result that the car was soon moved to Derby Castle for

Monday the 6th April was the first day of the 2009 season and to mark the occasion the first northbound service was operated by car No.21 and winter saloon trailer No.57. The pair are seen here near Ballaskeig, with just about 15 minutes to go before reaching Ramsey.

restoration.

The sad news of the death of former Director of Public Transport David Howard on the 15th May 2007 following a heart attack took no time to reach the Island and his funeral at Pevensey Church in West Sussex was attended by several representatives from Isle of Man Transport.

Services were disrupted for a while on the 3rd August following a road traffic accident in the Onchan area. Car 5 was damaged in a collision with a hedge trimmer during September and remained out of service awaiting winter repairs.

Station buildings at Baldrine, Fairy Cottage, South Cape and Minorca all received attention over the 2006/07 winter. Following an appeal by the Railway to local organisations

On 31st October 2007 car No.22 is nearing the summit while working alone from Ramsey to Derby Castle. The scenery on the northern section is superb, the village of Dhoon visible above the tram nestling on the lower slopes of Slieau Ruy.

Following the relaying of the track through Dhoon Glen station, the whole station area was tidied up with block paved areas and tarmac pathways, all in all making a very pleasing appearance. Car No.19 passes the station with a trailer in tow on 15th August 2008.

During the short season for the northern section of the line in 2008, a temporary passing loop was installed near Ballaskeig Halt. The loop was necessary due to the single line working, also requiring the use of single line Tickets. Here the driver of Car No.5 arrived first and is handing his Ticket to the driver of car No.21 operating towards Derby Castle on 15th August 2008.

The majority of the services north of Laxey are operated by the winter saloons backed up by the 1894 built tunnel cars. Green liveried car No.16 with trailer 60 are captured at Ballaskeig while working a service from Derby Castle to Ramsey. They were operating at the request of a group of enthusiasts. The superb scenery that surrounds the line in this area is clearly evident.

The actual summit of the line was until recently unmarked. However, the untimely death of Mike Goodwyn gave the Manx Electric Railway Society the opportunity to erect this memorial to him, at the summit of his favourite electric tramway. Mike was a motorman for many years and became known to all the enthusiasts who undertook the Motorman lessons that he tutored, during the various events of the 1990's.

Bertie the diesel at work on the Manx Electric. This locomotive has been on the Island for a number of years on loan to RMS Locotec and has been used extensively on the line during the relaying programme. It was captured here on the southbound running track at Dhoon Quarry on 10th April 2006 with a double hopper ballast wagon in tow. The wagon is constructed on the chassis of former steam railway coach F65.

and individuals to 'look after' shelters, Laxey School has volunteered to keep Minorca clean and tidy.

The former Ballaglass Power Station building, now converted into a private dwelling, was on the market for £2.85 million in early 2007.

Recent residential development in Ramsey has led to the sighting of a new request stop known as Queens Valley Road, the new stop becoming available in June 2007.

Passenger figures for the 2007 season showed that 78,665 were carried on the line, a 9.9% increase on the 2006 numbers.

The Laxey car shed replacement continues to be an issue with no progress being made. It was hoped that construction would start in the spring of 2008 but it now looks to be scheduled for late 2008 with completion in early 2009.

RMS Locotec carried out around 3? miles of track

replacement over the 2007/08 winter with a price tag in the region of £1.6 million. However an inspection of the line early in 2008 revealed a number of safety issues regarding sections of track yet to be replaced. The result was an announcement in Tynwald on the 20th February by the Minister of Tourism and Leisure that, the Manx Electric would not open between Laxey and Ramsey for the 2008 season.

As might have been expected, uproar ensued and by the 12th March Tynwald had agreed emergency funding to allow the issues on the landside track to be addressed immediately, with a view to having a single line operation over the northern section for the mid summer.

A further announcement by the Minister came on the 2nd July stating that the northern section would open to traffic on Saturday the 19th July and that a passing loop had been

The summit of North Barrule is covered by cloud as car No.6 works a through service from Ramsey to Derby Castle during the brief season for the northern section in 2008, The tram is working wrong line and will continue to do so until it reaches Laxey station. The village of Glen Mona is to the right of the tram.

Wagon number 21 in its latest guise. This wagon started life as an 1895 built power car, later having its bodywork removed and used as a flat wagon with hydraulic cranes on each end. It was later converted as shown here into a ballasting wagon, also seen, this time in the siding, at Dhoon Quarry on 31st October 2007.

The line reached the outskirts of Ramsey at Ballure in 1898 and terminated about where the Author is standing to take this picture. In 1899 the final section of line including this viaduct was opened taking the line to its current terminus in the centre of Ramsey. Working wrong line Car No.22 crosses Ballure Viaduct with a late afternoon service to Derby Castle on a rather dull 7th September 2008.

installed allowing an improved timetable over that which had been envisaged in March.

A small ceremony was held at Laxey on the 18th July prior to the departure of a special tram through to Ramsey, the line opening to the public the following day.

The single line operation worked well, with virtually a normal service operating. It ran until the 14th September when it closed again to allow track renewal work to restart. This work has been completed over the recent winter and the line will operate throughout with double track from the beginning of the 2009 season.

Meanwhile the old Laxey car shed was demolished at the end of the 2008 season, the site was cleared and by the middle of January 2009, construction of the replacement shed was well under way.

The 2009 season began on the 6th April, with trams using both tracks on the northern section and in line with the steam railway, the service level is reduced from the end of September through to the end of season in early November.

The Laxey car shed was completed in time for the opening of the line but was not actually connected. Work on the trackwork continues and the shed should be fully operational by the middle of the season.

Immediately the trams finished for the year, the section of track between the entrance to Derby Castle depot and the approach to Onchan Head station was relaid.

The need to empty the former Homefield bus garage in upper Douglas saw items of rolling stock returning to the line that had been absent since the rebuilding of the Derby Castle top shed.

In common with the steam railway the 2010 season dates were announced with services starting on the 20th March. In addition 'Ultimate Driving Experience' sessions were advertised allowing participants to drive trams between Laxey and Ramsey.

Having passed Queens Valley the line soon emerges alongside Walpole Road. Now running wrong line, Car No.9 heads into Ramsey with a service from Derby Castle on 1st September 2008. Notice that there are no centre poles, the overhead supported by poles to the left of the tracks. These poles were recovered from the Douglas Southern Electric Tramway when that line closed in 1939.

Mad Sunday TT 2007, the Ramsey Sprint is on and many thousands of people have descended on the town for the day. Many will have travelled on the Manx Electric and so in anticipation of their return, plenty of trams will be ready. Waiting patiently are winter saloon No.21 and open toastrack No.33 on Sunday the 3rd June 2007.

The superb condition of winter saloon trailers 57 and 58 is partly due to their little use. They are superb vehicles and a tribute to the craftsman who created them over a century ago.

THE GROUDLE GLEN RAILWAY

During the late 19th century Groudle Glen was being developed as a tourist attraction. A zoo was built at the mouth of the Glen along with a refreshment room, and a further refreshment room was constructed just below the headland loop. The Groudle Glen Railway was conceived to transport visitors from Lhen Coan station, situated near the entrance to the Glen, out to the refreshment rooms and zoo.

The 2ft gauge railway was constructed by local labour during 1895 and the early part of 1896. Spring 1896 saw the arrival of the railway's first locomotive, the Sea Lion and three 4-wheeled coaches. The railway opened to the public

The Groudle Glen railway was built to bring holidaymakers out to Sea Lion Rocks, so named because there were Sea Lions and Polar Bears in the small zoo adjacent to the station. The last trains ran to here in about 1939, when it re-opened after the Second World War the section from Headland to Sea Lion Rocks did not re-open. The restoration of the line brought trains back to the terminus in May 1992. Here we see Sea Lion with its train ready to depart for Lhen Coan on the day after services were restored.

on the 23rd May 1896, with 10,000 passengers being carried in the first two months and over 100,000 in the first three years, with up to 40 return trips being worked each day.

During the winter of 1904/05 a new longer shed was constructed at Lhen Coan station and a run-round loop installed at Headland, in readiness for the arrival in May 1905 of the second steam locomotive, the Polar Bear and four further coaches.

The outbreak of World War I caused the railway to close

but it soon reopened at the end of hostilities and visitors flooded back to the Glen. Sadly a steep rise in coal prices caused the two steam locomotives to be stored and replaced by battery electric machines. These proved troublesome, one of them finishing up at the bottom of the glen following an accident. After only six years the electrics were withdrawn and the two steam locomotives were overhauled by their builders and returned to service.

Over the years the line has had a number of visiting steam locomotives. One such visitor was this 0-4-0 named Chaloner from the Leighton Buzzard Railway. The visitor is seen here at Sea Lion Rocks with a full three coach train.

World War II caused the railway to close once again, not reopening until 1950, and then only to the Headland because of a serious rockfall between there and Sea Lion Rocks. The Polar Bear was the only serviceable locomotive, with six coaches available. A small petrol locomotive was tried out on the line as a spare but soon disappeared as it was too weak for the gradients and uncontrollable on downward sections. The 1950s saw a decline in the number of visitors and an irregular service operated.

A change of ownership of the glen in 1960 resulted in a revival, with the Polar Bear and the six coaches operating with regular services until the end of the 1962 season.

Below: In early 1998 planning permission was eventually received to re-instate the refreshment facility at Sea Lion Rocks. The building acts as a cafeteria and a shop and provides welcome shelter on windy days.

Below: On a bright sunny 5 July 2009 Annie awaits departure from Sea Lion Rocks with a train of bogie coaches. Driver Alex Brindley enjoys a well earned break while discussing the locomotives controls with two young enthusiasts.

Below: In July 2004 the railway took delivery of a replica of one of the original British Electric Vehicles (BEV) electric locomotives. The replica was converted by Alan Keefe, from a locomotive built by BEV in the 1990's. The replica named Polar Bear is seen here in the company of Sea Lion at Sea Lion Rocks terminus on 16th July 2006.

Below: On a sunny day in May 2008, Sea Lion stands at Sea Lion Rocks station after arrival from Lhen Coan. The scenery on the outer section of the line is difficult to beat. No doubt the passengers are enjoying an ice cream from the café, while the crew will be preparing for the return trip.

One of the original new bogie coaches built for the line in 1984 on the frames of one of the original Dodington chassis. It is seen here between trains at Sea Lion Rocks in July 2006.

Not every railway operates an ice cream train. Battery electric locomotive Polar Bear passes the Headland loop with the ice cream cooler returning to Lhen Coan after a days operation in July 2006. No doubt on a hot day like this, the cooler is virtually empty.

The superb scenery is clearly evident in this view of Sea Lion heading towards Lhen Coan with the three replica original coaches. The authentic Groudle train has just left Sea Lion Rocks, the station building clearly visible, as is the run round loop.

When the line was re-laid from Headland to Sea Lion Rocks the headland was dug back, the new track being about six feet further inland than the original line. Despite the 17 years since the work was completed the exposed bank has still yet to produce vegetation. Sea Lion heads towards Headland and Lhen Coan with a short train on 16th July 2006.

Sea Lion leads two coaches round the curve that represents the end of the 1992 extension and rejoins the first length of restored line in this July 2006 view.

Easter Bunny specials are a feature of the lines season. Here complete with special headboard, Sea Lion leads a three coach train banked by Annie round the double curve shortly after passing the headland loop. A recent addition to many of the items of rolling stock is the crest displayed here on the sides of the passenger coaches.

During the 1962/63 winter a good deal of repair work was carried out and attempts were made to purchase a second-hand locomotive but none could be found. The 1963 season came and went but the railway was unable to operate any trains, due to the failure of the Polar Bear. The 'old' railway never reopened.

In 1965 the Groudle Glen Railway Preservation Society was formed. At first things looked promising but in 1967 the owners of the Glen ordered the removal of all railway equipment, with the result that, by June 1968, the locomotives and rolling stock were dispersed all over the British Isles. The Sea Lion and a few coaches managed to stay on the Island, being exhibited at the Steam Centre in Kirk Michael and these items were left behind when, in the late 1970s, the Steam Centre closed down and moved to the newly established Midlands Steam Centre at Loughborough.

trackbed of fallen trees, gorse and bracken being the first job. A borrowed mechanical digger meant that what would have been months of clearing work was completed in a matter of weeks, while a smaller digger was used to dig trenches for new drains to be installed.

A few 4-wheeled wagons formerly used at RAF Fauld, Staffordshire were purchased and arrived on the Island in October 1982. Spring 1983 saw the purchase of the entire Dodington Narrow Gauge Railway, situated near Chipping Sodbury, Avon, which had gone into voluntary liquidation. This provided two diesel locomotives, two coaches plus a spare coach frame, two points and 1,080 yards of track.

The works plate of Polar Bear.

A close up of the replica works plate of battery electric locomotive Polar Bear. Recently found documentation has identified which makers number was carried by each of the two locomotives.

This little line had surely gone for good.

The Sea Lion Locomotive Association was formed in 1981, eventually moving their locomotive to Loughborough in October 1981, where it was cosmetically restored.

In January 1982 the Isle of Man Steam Railway Supporters' Association embarked on what must be one of the most impressive narrow gauge railway restorations ever. Structural surveys were carried out and it was agreed that to reinstate the railway was possible, providing the original formation was kept. The new owners of the Glen and the Manx Government gave full support, and planning permission was received in May 1982.

The Supporters' Association members needed no further encouragement and restoration work started, clearing the

The Sea Lion was also the subject of negotiations with her owners and it was agreed that the Association could complete the restoration, on which little progress had been made at Loughborough, and operate the locomotive for as long as they continued to run the railway. This locomotive returned to the Island in March 1983. Meanwhile, in the glen, 150 tons of ballast had been delivered and tracklaying was completed from Headland to Lime Kiln Halt.

Towards the end of 1983, the volunteers could wait no longer. They set up a Santa's grotto in the engine shed at Headland and on the 18th December 550 people rode between Lime Kiln Halt and the grotto, the first passengers to travel on the line for 21 years. Two of the Fauld wagons were used, hauled by one of the diesel locomotives, specially named the Rudolph for the day. Boxing Day saw more Santa specials and a further 200 visitors.

Tracklaying had reached half way to Lhen Coan by mid

Sea Lion passing the Headland loop with a train bound for Sea Lion Rocks on a bright sunny 16th July 2006. The two locally built coaches have a good load of passengers on board. The siding behind the locomotive leads to the area used to load and unload rolling stock and place it onto the track.

Approaching Lime Kiln Halt while working towards Sea Lion Rocks is Sea Lion with a short train of bogie stock on 16th July 2006. Between Lime Kiln and Lhen Coan the line runs along a ledge on the north side of the Glen, the passengers enjoying a view of the river below.

Shortly before arriving at Lhen Coan station passengers get a look at the main rolling stock sheds. Former Dodington Hunslett diesel, now named Walrus, is captured taking a rest with one of the bogie coaches, outside the shed during May 2008.

Below: Early in 2002 the railway purchased this former Ministry of Defence brake van and after the removal of ballast weight, the vehicle was repainted into this red livery and now forms part of the works train, along with a bogie wagon.

Below: Former Dodington railway Hunslett diesel locomotive, now Groudle No.2 Walrus is seen shunting the brake van back into its shed, from where it had been specially extracted to have its picture taken. The bogie works wagon can be seen on the siding to the right of the shed.

Below: A general view of the approach to Lhen Coan station. The shed in the foreground was built during the initial preservation project in 1986; the new (2008) engine shed is visible to the left, with the station beyond.

Below: A closer view of the bogie works wagon, constructed using parts obtained from the former Quiggins timber yard at Douglas. It is seen here parked round the back of the sheds at Lhen Coan.

Inside the main shed are the three replica 4-wheeled coaches and one of the bogie coaches behind. The protection offered by this sort of storage is invaluable when wooden stock is employed on a railway.

A view of the new locomotive shed constructed during the 2008 season and designed to replicate the original shed, that had collapsed by the time the preservation team got to work in the Glen.

1984 and, as the Apprentice Training Centre at BNFL Sellafield had offered to carry out all remaining restoration work on the Sea Lion, the locomotive left the Island once again in October 1984 bound for Cumbria. Autumn that year saw considerable efforts made to complete the tracklaying as far as Lhen Coan station, which was duly achieved in readiness for a repeat of the Santa trains. The second diesel locomotive was delivered to the line, along with the first coach, built on one of the former Dodington underframes. The two diesels were named Dolphin and Walrus and the Yuletide running was another outstanding success.

Work continued through 1985, a wet summer delaying further deliveries of ballast, while Tynwald passed the Groudle Glen Railway Order which meant that the railway had to be inspected before any more passengers could be

During the hugely successful events of the 1990's, the Groudle Glen railway also staged a number of night photography sessions. On one such occasion in 1993, the two original Groudle locomotives, Polar Bear and Sea Lion are seen together outside the shed at the end of the evening.

carried. The inspector called in November and issued a pass certificate, opening the way for 1,300 people to visit the line over Christmas.

February 1986 saw the steelwork for the new shed arrive in the Glen and, by the end of March, the 20ft by 50ft steel framework was in place. A second coach was delivered and the temporary wooden shed was moved underneath the steelwork of the new one.

On the 25th May 1986, to the delight of the Isle of Man Steam Railway Supporters' Association volunteers and to the sound of Rushen Silver Band, the Dolphin was driven through a white tape, by Mrs Carolyn Rawson, daughter of the late Dennis Jeavons who had conceived and developed

the Groudle Glen holiday village. After 24 years the Groudle Glen Railway was now officially open again, probably in better condition than it had ever been before. Trains ran every Sunday for the rest of the year, the Santa trains attracting 1,600 people.

Early 1987 was spent completing the new running shed, ready for the season, the highlight of which was the return of the Sea Lion to the railway on the 8th September.

Steam was raised for the first time in 25 years on the 21st September and an official handing over ceremony took place on the 3rd October. The now annual Santa specials were steam hauled for the first time.

Another picture outside the shed on the occasion of the naming of a former resident locomotive. It was about to be named Jack and is being prepared for its big day by its owner Richard Booth. The locomotive has since been sold and has moved off the Island.

Restoration work continued between running trains with, in 1988, the completion of run-round facilities at Lhen Coan and thoughts turning to the reinstatement of the line to Sea Lion Rocks. Cosmetic work included a start on the building of a replica station canopy at Lhen Coan, completed in time for the 'Year of Railways' in 1993.

During late 1990, after much negotiation and the purchase of a strip of land from a local farmer, work started on the extension of the line to its original terminus at Sea Lion Rocks. A mechanical digger was called in once again to shift tons of soil, moving the railway ledge further inland. Tracklaying commenced in early 1991, continuing throughout the year and on into 1992. New fences were erected around the cliff edges at Sea Lion Rocks to prevent any accidents, the finishing touches being made to the trackwork during March. Diesel locomotive No.1 Dolphin

Below: Sea Lion enjoys a well earned break inside the new shed during the last few weeks of the 2008 season. The shed has a pit area to allow easier access to the underside of the locomotives for maintenance. The sign on the far left of the picture reminds us of the joke about it taking hours to untangle them!

Below: A recent arrival at Groudle is this former Lyn-Barn Railway 0-4-0 steam outline diesel locomotive. Built by Baguley of Burton upon Trent in 1947, restoration is now underway and the locomotive will join the operating fleet at Groudle in due course.

Steam locomotives burn lots of coal. Transported to the glen by road, the coal is then transferred onto these wagons for the final part of the journey to Lhen Coan. Here a large stack is seen on one of the former RAF Fauld wagons in the siding at the terminus during August 2006. This area is now the site of the new locomotive shed.

Below: Inside the cab of Sea Lion are two plates, one reminding us that the locomotive was rebuilt by apprentices at Sellafield before returning to the restored railway in 1987, the second commemorating the life of Alistair Lamberton, one of the group behind the restoration of the line in the early 1980's.

Below: The commemorative plaque on the side of the new locomotive shed.

During 2008 a complete set of new station nameboards were completed, the first one actually displayed was at Lhen Coan. Each of the tree stations on the line will have these new boards for the 2009 season.

operated a test run over the new track on the 29th March, following which permission was given by the Railway Inspector for public services to commence.

Test runs in early April brought the return of the Sea Lion to the terminus for the first time in 53 years, with public services commencing on Easter Sunday, the 19th April. The extension was officially reopened on Saturday the 23rd May 1992 by Mr James Cain, Speaker of the House of Keys and Chairman of the Manx Heritage Foundation, the 96th anniversary of the railway first opening to the public.

The other Groudle steam locomotive, the Polar Bear restored to full working order at the Amberley Chalk Pits Museum in West Sussex made a triumphant return to the Groudle Glen Railway for August and September 1993 as part of the centenary celebrations for the Manx Electric.

The Polar Bear had left the Island in 1967, going to the now closed Brockham Museum in Surrey, where restoration commenced. Following the transfer of much of the equipment from there to the Amberley Chalk Pits Museum in West Sussex, this work was completed and it saw occasional operation subsequently, alongside many other interesting narrow gauge railway exhibits. A further complete overhaul was completed in July 1993, prior to its visit to the Island.

The replica overall station roof at Lhen Coan was completed in early 1993 and at the request of the Railway Inspector, substantial barriers were erected at Sea Lion Rocks to prevent passengers falling over the steep cliff edges.

The visit of the Polar Bear along with three original style 4-wheeled coaches no doubt contributed to the 13,000 passengers carried on the railway in 1993, a 136% increase on the previous year.

A third new bogie coach entered service, while electric lighting was installed at Lhen Coan for the sheds and station.

Two visiting locomotives the Rishra and the Chaloner operated on the railway for part of the 1995 season, as part of the 'International Railway Festival' celebrating the centenary of the Snaefell Mountain Railway. A new loop was installed at Headland during the 1995/96 winter.

The Sea Lion was moved to the Steam Railway workshops in Douglas on the 7th October 1995 for its ten year overhaul, while plans were in hand for the Groudle's own centenary in 1996 and another visit of the Polar Bear.

The Sea Lion went on a tour on the mainland during May 1997 visiting the Festiniog Railway, Amerton Farm Railway in Staffordshire and the Leighton Buzzard Railway, operating service trains at the latter two. The Sea Lion returned to service at Groudle on the 1st June.

Work on a second replica 4-wheeled coach got underway at the workshops of Harold Flavell towards the end of 1997, this along with the first replica and the coach from Lytham St Anne's will make up a train of three as used on the railway.

Also nearing completion was a replica of 1911 W. G. Bagnall locomotive the Annie, and following testing she made her first passenger trip on the 28th June. Visiting

In brilliant sunshine Sea Lion rounds the curve just beyond the Headland loop with a Sea Lion Rocks bound train on 18th May 2008. In the distance the Isle of Man Steam Packet vessel Viking heads for Heysham. The light load on the three original style coaches indicates that this is the last train of the day.

Below: During its 1993 visit, Polar Bear arrives at Lhen Coan with a train of replica and rebuilt 4-wheeled coaches, no doubt with enthusiasts from all over the world as passengers. One of the former RAF Fauld wagons rests in the siding.

Below: Polar Bear awaiting departure from Lhen Coan with a train of 4-wheeled coaches. The superb replica station roof has now been joined by other buildings, including a new shop installed during the recent winter.

Below: Lhen Coan terminus on 25th May 1986 as final preparations are made for the official opening of the preserved line. Locomotive No.1 Dolphin is poised to do the honours and crowds gather to witness this special occasion. The locomotive was driven through the tape by Mrs Carolyn Rawson daughter of the late Dennis Jeavons, founder of the holiday village.

Below: Construction of locomotive Annie started in Laxey but, when assembly started the locomotive was too big for that workshop and so space was borrowed within the Steam Railway workshops at Douglas station. In order for the locomotive to be tested, a short length of 2'0" gauge track was laid outside the shed. Annie is seen here in steam outside the shed, a picture that surely proves that dogs are interested in steam trains!

Sea Lion stands at the head of the three bogie coaches with Annie on the back, ready to return to Lime Kiln Halt with another train load of children who have just had their last chance to put their requests to Santa Claus, before the big day arrives. Captured on 23rd December 2006.

Visiting locomotives Peter Pan and Jonathan stand at Lhen Coan during a break in activities in 1996, the year the line celebrated its centenary. A special centenary plaque can be seen in the apex of the station roof. The shop to the left of the picture has been replaced during the recent winter with a walk in version.

locomotives for the 1998 season were the Jonathan and the Peter Pan.

The second Flavell-built replica 1896 style coach entered service on the 8th May 1998 and a third was started. After much negotiation, planning consent was received for a building at Sea Lion Rocks on the site of the original 1896 structure. Work on the building started soon after consent was received. Later in May the railway mourned the sudden death of the steam engineer and long-term member Alistair Lamberton.

The Sea Lion, having completed 15 years' service was treated to a full overhaul and new boiler at the Ross-on-Wye works of Alan Keefe Ltd, at the beginning of the 2002 season. The following winter the locomotive lost its light green livery in favour of a Brunswick green.

The line's motive power fleet enjoyed the addition of a replica of one of the BEV electric locomotives, converted at the works of Alan Keefe from a 1990's built battery electric locomotive from the same manufacturer as the originals. It was inaugurated on the 8th August 2004 and named Polar Bear.

Before being transported to the Island the replica was exhibited at the York Railfest from the 28th May to the 6th June, arriving on the Railway on the 7th July. The line played host to visiting locomotive the Taffy from the collection of Patrick and Alan Keefe later the same month.

The station at Lime Kiln received a new shelter over the 2004/05 winter and the whole area was tidied up and enhanced.

The year 2005 marked the 100th birthday of original Groudle locomotive Polar Bear, now at the Amberley Chalk Pits Museum in Sussex. To celebrate the occasion it was arranged that the Island-based the Sea Lion should travel to Amberley at the beginning of July, returning on the 16th July with the Polar Bear, the latter spending two weeks at Groudle before returning home to Sussex.

The third replica 4-wheeled coach arrived at Groudle from the workshops of Harold Flavell on the 22nd July 2005.

Relaying and replacement of the former Donnington rail saw the section between Blue Lagoon and Lime Kiln Halt completed during the 2006/07 winter. A new steam outline diesel locomotive arrived on the line in early 2007.

Planning permission was sought for the construction of a new locomotive shed at Lhen Coan in February 2007. Based on the original design the 9m x 4.8m and 4.03m high two track shed would have a concrete floor with pits and a workshop area.

Work on the new engine shed started soon after planning permission had been received. The main structure was supplied by Kingsland Stabling of Leominster and was completed and erected by them on site in June 2007. The shed was officially opened later that summer.

The year 2007 marked the 25th anniversary of the beginning of the restoration of the line, and by way of a celebration a special running day was held during August.

The railway has adopted a newly designed crest, similar in appearance to that of the Isle of Man Railway and used for the Groudle centenary. Transfers have been applied to the sides of most items of stock.

At the end of 2007 Harold Flavell a stalwart of the restoration of the line, finally retired. Sadly just a few months later Harold died at his home aged 80. He was responsible for the construction of all the early sheds and equipment boxes, the booking office, shop, catering unit and many other smaller items for the restored railway. The second and third red bogie coaches came from his workshop as did the three replica 4-wheeled coaches, utilising as many original metal parts as possible. He had finished fabricating the parts for a fourth 4-wheeler.

Throughout 2008 preparations were made for the installation of a new shop at Lhen Coan, the building arriving on the site in kit form towards the end of the season. Amongst the regular track maintenance during the winter the new building was put together and finished off, providing a walk in shop as apposed to the kiosk style it replaced.

On the 6th March 2009, just as the beginning of the new season was in sight, the news broke of the death of Tony Beard. Tony had for nearly 30 years been the voice of Groudle and was one of the original band of enthusiasts who believed that it could be done. Indeed it could and Tony was always there in the thick of it and there is no doubt that he will be sadly missed down in the Glen.

The line enjoyed a buoyant season with passenger numbers up on 2008, the new shop was partially opened in July while plans to extend the Sea Lion Rocks building were announced.

The summer evening operation was combined with the Manx Electric service and through tickets offered, a combination that worked well.

Shortly after the season ended track relaying commenced, stopping for the annual Santa trains, while plans for the 2010 timetable include operating on Saturdays in the high summer as well as on Sundays.

THE SNAEFELL MOUNTAIN RAILWAY

The idea of a railway to the summit of the Island's highest mountain first surfaced in 1888, when Tynwald was asked to approve a plan submitted by the Douglas, Laxey & Snaefell Railway to build a steam-operated line. Mr J.B. Fell, the inventor of the 'Fell Incline Railway System', was behind the project but nothing ever came of it.

The arrival in Laxey of the Manx Electric Railway in 1894 renewed interest in Mr Fell's ideas and, on the 4th January 1895, The Snaefell Mountain Railway Association met in Douglas for the first time and announced its intention to build a line from Laxey to near the summit of Snaefell. The syndicate included several members of the Isle of Man Tramways & Electric Power Co., including Mr Bruce of Dumbells Bank and Mr Fell. Discussions were held about motive power and the association decided on an electric

tramway. The route of the line was nearly all on Crown property, which avoided the need for an Act of Tynwald before construction could begin. In order to incorporate the 'Fell System' between the wheels the line would be constructed to 3' 6" gauge, six inches wider than the Island's standard. Manx Northern Railway locomotive No.4 Caledonia was borrowed to assist with construction trains, necessitating the laying of a temporary 3' 0" gauge rail.

Construction of the line started in January 1895, with bad weather during February delaying the project by about a month, but by early August completion was near. Six trams were delivered from G.F. Milnes, while Mather & Platt supplied the overhead equipment, that was erected along the entire length of the line in just ten days, the wire being 16ft above rail level.

The first day of service for 2008 was 28th April. Taken the day after, car No.2 has recently arrived, its passengers now forming an orderly queue in the café, while the few braver ones walk to the summit. The pylons on the summit provide a variety of services including air traffic control for aircraft entering UK air space from across the Atlantic. The actual summit is just above the right hand end of the tram.

Below: During the centenary year a number of events were staged, perhaps the most impressive being this tram convoy from the Summit to Bungalow. All six trams were assembled at the Summit station and then all descended to Bungalow, three on each track and as evenly spaced as possible. This view shows the six cars all in the same picture as they approach Bungalow.

Below: During the 1995 celebrations hundreds were transported up the mountain one evening in a convoy of trams, the café was open and the whole event had a carnival atmosphere about it. Car No.5 is seen here at just before midnight as its crew tried to gather a tram load of passengers before departing for Laxey.

The Air Traffic control equipment at the summit has at intervals to be upgraded. On one such occasion in 2006 the state of the art replacement computers were transported to the summit on this wagon propelled by a 111 year old tramcar. The wagon was left for unloading and collected later.

Below: On the penultimate day of operation for the 2008 season, car No.5 is seen shortly after arrival at the summit station. Car No.5 differs from the rest of the fleet in not having a clerestory roof. The original 1895 built car caught fire at this summit station on 16th August 1970, the rebuilt car having a conventional roof.

Below: On 21st August 1995 the then Governor of the Isle of Man, Air Marshall Sir Laurence Jones unveiled a plaque in the hotel to mark the completion of its refurbishment. The Governor is seen here shortly after the ceremony.

A little while later car No.5 was back with some rather larger items on the same truck and is seen here just short of the terminus. This tram carries the lines name on its sides in Manx.

The weather on the summit can vary considerably from day to day, even within the same day. Seen here ascending the final stretch of the line is car No.4 on a misty morning in September 2008. The mountain in the background is Clagh Ouyr.

Having left Bungalow on the ascent, the line runs in a circle round the mountain as it gains height. On a misty day, car No.6 is ascending the mountain from Laxey and Bungalow.

A telephoto shot of car No.6 descending towards and approaching Bungalow on the penultimate day of the 2008 season.

Under blue skies but with cloud blocking the sunshine, Car No.6 is nearing Bungalow on its descent from the Summit to Laxey. The journey will take around 30 minutes and shortly after arrival in Laxey the tram will be on its way back up again.

Car No.5 approaches Bungalow station with a service for Laxey on 27th September 2008. This picture was taken from the top of the TT access bridge, used when racing is in progress to get passengers from one side of the course to the other. During racing trams operate in two sections to either side of the Mountain Road at Bungalow.

The new Bungalow station building is to the left of the picture, the old facility visible above the tram as No.5 begins the second stage of its descent from the summit to Laxey. The tram is crossing the A18 Mountain Road, part of the world famous TT circuit. The line to the Summit can be seen above the tram.

The 4 mile 53 chain line was completed in record time, the Fell rail being laid midway between the running rails. However, during construction, it was proved elsewhere that an electric tramcar could climb a 1 in 9 gradient without assistance and so the Fell equipment was never fitted to the cars. This third rail is therefore only used for friction braking in the event of a runaway.

Testing was carried out in mid August and the line was officially opened from the first Laxey station, situated alongside the present car sheds, to the Summit station 1,990ft above sea level, on the 20th August 1895, with the first public services the following day. An average of 900 passengers a day were carried with the six cars operating a ten-minute service.

The cars, which were delivered unglazed, similar to the Manx Electric Nos.10 to 13 series, received sliding glazed windows in 1896 and clerestory roofs during the winter of 1896/97, to provide ventilation on hot days.

In December 1895 the Association sold the entire line to the Isle of Man Tramways & Electric Power Co. for £72,500, which was £32,500 more than it had cost to build.

The original Summit Hotel, located a little to the south of the terminus, was extended in 1896 and a new hotel was built at Halfway, now known as Bungalow.

The Isle of Man Tramways & Electric Power Co. considered the distance between their coastal line station and the Snaefell station in Laxey to be too great. The Snaefell

terminus was therefore moved to the end of Dumbells Row in 1897, and in 1898 a further move brought it into the same station as the coastal line, as is still the case.

The Snaefell line was sold to the Manx Electric Railway Co. in 1902, following the collapse of Dumbells Bank. In common with the coastal line, much re-equipping was needed and changes were made to the generation and distribution of electricity.

The only serious incident on the line occurred on the 14th September 1905, when three cars were descending in convoy. The first stalled, the second stopped without difficulty but the third failed to stop, colliding with the second and pushing it forward into the first. All three cars were damaged and a number of passengers injured.

The line continued to be a considerable success and the hotel at the summit proved inadequate to cope with the vast numbers of passengers. In order to overcome this, an elaborate new hotel was built alongside the railway terminus, opening in 1906.

A note in Isle of Man Tramways & Electric Power Co. documents of 1897 considered the possibility of a line from Bungalow to Tholt-y-Will but nothing ever came of this. In 1907 however, following the construction of a hotel and refreshment room at Tholt-y-Will, the Manx Electric Railway Co. started a motor charabanc service over this route, generally regarded as the first motor bus service on the Island. This and mountain railway services ceased at the

Another spectacle of the 1995 centenary celebrations was the return to steam on former Manx Northern Locomotive No.4 Caledonia, now No.15 in the Isle of Man Railway fleet. An extra rail was installed on the inner track from Bungalow to the Summit to allow the 3'0" gauge locomotive to operate on the mountain line. Here the locomotive is seen setting off from Bungalow with Manx Electric trailer No.58, bound for the Summit.

The multi coloured hillsides of the Laxey Valley form the backdrop to this view of car No.4 approaching Bungalow and about to cross the Mountain Road. The crossover in the foreground is used during racing to allow cars to turn back without crossing the road. A similar crossover is installed on the other side of the road.

Pictures of trams between Bungalow and Laxey are rare, due mainly to the difficult terrain. However with perseverance it is possible to get to the line on this stretch. Here we see car No.4 descending from the mountain below the slopes of Cronk y Vaare. The former motorcycle museum building is visible by the top of the overhead pole to the right of the tram.

outbreak of World War I.

Following the end of hostilities and the clearing of arrears of maintenance, the line reopened on the 10th June 1919. The Tholt-y-Will service also restarted but with different vehicles, as the charabancs had been sold. Two Ford Model Ts took over in 1926 and these, in turn, gave way to Bedford coaches in 1939.

All rail and road services were stopped on the 20th September 1939, soon after the outbreak of World War II, but the line saw some traffic after this, carrying peat down to Laxey from the Bungalow area to assist with fuel shortages. This traffic was handled by freight car No. 7, nicknamed Maria, with bogies borrowed from passenger car No. 5.

The post-war boom in the tourist industry on the Island provided the line with plenty of passengers and frequent

Passenger numbers continued to fall and in 1953 the coach service to Tholt-y-Will was withdrawn. At the end of the 1955 season the Manx Electric Railway Co. advised the Government that it would be unable to operate the railway after the end of the following year. However, a nationalisation agreement was reached and the Manx Electric Railway Board took control of the line on the 1st June 1957.

The Tholt-y-Will coach service was reinstated but with little patronage, was extended to Sulby the following year and soon abandoned altogether. The Summit Hotel was redecorated in 1958, whilst the Bungalow Hotel was closed

The mountain lines flat wagon captured between duties at Bungalow. This wagon is built onto 1895 passenger car bogie sideframes following their renewal as part of the rebuild programme of the late 1970's.

2007 marked the centenary of the first motor bus services on the Island, operated by the Manx Electric Railway from Bungalow to Tholt-y-Will and Sulby. On Saturday 21 July as part of a weekend of celebration, the Manx Transport Trust organised some special re-enactment trips from Bungalow to the Sulby Reservoir, weight limits preventing the buses going any further. Richard Davis provided his superb preserved Isle of Man Road Services Leyland Leopard No.97 and in order to cope with demand, Isle of Man Transport produced a fully licensed Dennis Dart. The Leopard is seen at Bungalow in the company of Snaefell Car No.5.

services were operated. Visitor numbers began to dwindle in the early 1950s but a decision by the Air Ministry (later the Civil Aviation Authority) to construct a radar station at the summit provided work for the line during the winter of 1950/51. The radar station presented a problem in that it had become customary to remove the overhead wire from the upper section in winter to avoid it becoming damaged. As the Ministry would need the line all year, it purchased a Wickham railcar in 1951 and a second in 1957. These were, and the current railcars are housed in a small shed on the Snaefell depot site.

and demolished. Cars 2 and 4 were repainted into a new livery of green and cream but this was soon abandoned. No. 4 was the last car of either of the mountain and coastal lines so treated.

The entire line showed signs of age and corrosion by the mid 1960s, the Fell rail being of particular concern. Whilst the track was receiving attention, the cars themselves were becoming in desperate need of mechanical and electrical overhaul and, between 1958 and 1975, several possible solutions were considered and rejected for various reasons.

Disaster struck on the 16th August 1970 when, shortly after arrival at the Summit station on a particularly windy day, car No.5 caught fire and was almost completely destroyed. It was later discovered that a high tension cable had rubbed on the chassis and worn through. Interestingly the high wind meant that some of the paint on the Laxey end of the car was not even scorched. Despite offers of a modern design of car body for the original chassis, the Manx

A couple of minutes after leaving Bungalow on the descent to Laxey the trams pass the former generating station and latterly electricity sub station. Passing on its way to the Summit is car No.6. To the left of the tram is what remains of one of the old boilers from the power station. The summit of Slieau Ruy is just visible at the top of the picture.

The village of Agneash is just about visible with The Dreem behind as car No.5 makes a steady ascent of the mountain high above the Laxey Valley. The track from Agneash up to the old Snaefell Mine is also visible on the other side of the valley.

Electric Railway Board thankfully decided to rebuild the car in its original form, although aluminium bus-style windows replaced the sliding wooden type of the original body. H.D. Kinnan of Ramsey built the new body and the car re-entered service on the 8th July 1971.

The mechanical and electrical equipment on the cars was still giving serious cause for concern by the mid 1970s when the Manx Electric Railway Board called in London Transport to look at overhauling the cars' electrical equipment. They recommended that the equipment be replaced, possibly from second-hand trams if a suitable supply could be found. In May 1976 a batch of suitable donors was found in Aachen in Germany. Six trams, Nos.1003/04/05/08/09/11, were shipped to London Transport Lots Road Power Station works and the seventh, number 1010, made the journey to Douglas, laden with a good stock of spare parts. The trams were stripped of the required components and the six in London were then broken up. No. 1010 remained in use as a store until 1985, when it too was broken up.

London Transport had suggested that the Snaefell line gauge be changed to one metre to enable the Aachen bogies to be used as purchased. In the event, London Transport built 12 new bogies to the original Snaefell design, using only the Fell gear from the old bogies; the wheels, motors etc coming from the Aachen trams. The first pair of new bogies arrived at Laxey in April 1977, to be united with car No. I which began tests in May 1977 and entered service in June. The other five cars were similarly rebuilt over the next two years.

A number of minor modifications have since been carried out, including new wheels for all six cars, after it was found that the finer profile of the Aachen wheels caused problems on the Snaefell track.

Fire returned to the summit on the night of the 5/6th August 1982, this time gutting the hotel, the clearing-up operation resulting in the line being closed until the 9th August. To assist with the reconstruction, a crossover was installed just short of the station to enable the cars to terminate without having to go alongside the building. Two old 1895 bogie frames were fitted with small wagon bodies to assist in the conveyance of building materials to the hotel, which reopened for the 1984 season.

As the 1980s drew to a close, plans were announced to rebuild the car sheds at Laxey, to enable all maintenance work to be carried out there, without the need to haul the cars to Derby Castle. The old shed was demolished at the end of the 1994 season, the cars being housed in a temporary structure within the station area. The new shed

was completed in early 1995. The level crossing at Bungalow was rebuilt following the end of summer services in 1997.

The outbreak of Foot and Mouth on the Mainland, during 2001, led to many restrictions and closed footpaths on the Island, including the short path from the Summit station to the actual summit of Snaefell.

The upgrading of the facilities for staff and passengers at Bungalow was the subject of a planning application in 2002. Construction commenced over the winter of 2002/03, the new building to include a new substation, waiting area and staff quarters.

The long-term refurbishment of car 5 was completed in time for the 2003 season, the most notable and welcome change being the replacement of the bus-style windows with wooden sliding ones and the addition of Manx lettering on the sides of the tram.

A replica of the withdrawn No.7 Maria was hauled to Derby Castle in June 2003 where conversion to a 3'0" gauge works car was to take place. The locomotive emerged from the works with a centrally mounted generator, numbered 34 and painted yellow, with diagonal black lines on the ends.

Services on the line were suspended for a few days just after the start of the 2005 season, after a road vehicle damaged the overhead at Bungalow on the 26th April, the line reopening on the 29th April. Track was damaged and ballast washed away during a downpour in October 2005 but, as the line was closed no services were disrupted.

The Laxey road crossing was relaid along with that of the Manx Electric over the winter of 2005/06. The opportunity was taken to relay some of the Laxey station track. The dual gauge siding was retained.

Bad weather brought down the wires on the upper section in the early part of April 2006 and the line only operated as far as Bungalow on opening day, the 24th April; the first car to the Summit station operated on the 6th May.

A long term overhaul of car 3 continued throughout the 2006 season. An advert in the local press called for tenders to manufacture and supply 10km of Fell rail, with expressions of interest required by the 7th July. The new Fell rail was rolled in China and delivered to the Island during the early months of 2007.

A severe thunderstorm on the 22nd June 2007 caused services to be suspended as the risk of a lightning strike was considered too high to continue.

The footpath to the summit from the hotel was closed for a short while from the 3rd August following a further outbreak of Foot and Mouth on the mainland, while the hotel building itself received new rendering and a fresh coat of paint during the operating season, this due to the

Below: During the centenary year a number of photo stop trams operated, stopping at unusual places on the way to the summit. One such stop was at the sub station, from where car No.6 was captured operating down to Laxey with a demonstration wiring train. These wooden wiring trolleys are in the process of being replaced.

Below: The original Snaefell Railway car shed at Laxey was demolished in 1995 to make way for a modern facility that includes a workshop area. This is the old shed photographed shortly before demolition commenced. A collection of flat and tower wagons occupy the adjacent siding.

Below: One of the former Lochaber Railway flat wagons purchased primarily for the steam railway was re-gauged for use on the mountain line. It is seen here parked in the depot area at Laxey with a water tank as its load.

The CAA requires access to the air traffic control equipment on the summit, all year round. Two Wickam railcars are used during the winter months, a derelict example seen here at the Laxey depot is now preserved.

The new car shed was completed in time for the 1995 season and provides far superior storage for these century and a bit old trams. Resting between duties in the running shed is car No.1 on 27th September 2008.

The other half of the shed forms a workshop area where heavy maintenance and overhaul can be carried out. This work was traditionally done at derby Castle but is now carried out at Laxey. Nearing completion after a two year rebuild is car No.3 in the well equipped workshop.

Passing the depot while operating towards Laxey is car No.1 on 20th September 2008. In just a few yards the two tracks join up and the single line continues into the station.

difficulties of working on the summit in winter.

Track relay and Fell rail replacement took place over the winter of 2007/08 in several areas, some by contractors and other stretches by the local staff.

The line had a good season in 2008, helped no doubt by the high standards set in the Summit Café by the tenant.

One wonders if the engineers who built the Snaefell Mountain Railway nearly 114 years ago, thought that it would still be operating, largely in its original form in the 21st Century.

The line had a good season in 2008, helped no doubt by the high standards set in the Summit Café by the tenant.

Passenger numbers for both the 2008 and 2009 seasons held up well, the latter again no doubt assisted by the good grub in the hotel. The final day of the 2009 season was one of the best days of the year, the early mist over the mountain soon clearing and resulting in high numbers of passengers turning up for a last trip.

Further fell rail replacement and re-sleepering is planned for the current winter and it is hoped to return car No.3 to service after its extended overhaul.

With the 2010 season set to start on 24 April, one wonders if the engineers who built the Snaefell Mountain Railway nearly 115 years ago, ever imagined that it would still be operating, largely in its original form in the 21st Century.

The remains of former Aachen tramcar 1010, the one of seven similar trams bought in 1976 to refurbish the electrical equipment on the Snaefell fleet. Six other trams went to Lots Road in London, while 1010 travelled to the Island loaded with other spares for use on the Island.

Below: Isle of Man Railways have always attempted to attract the younger generation by decorating trains and trams to represent fictional characters. On one such occasion, an unidentified Snaefell car was decorated as Harold the tram.

Below: In 1896 G F Milnes built a twin cab locomotive for the line that borrowed power bogies from one of the passenger cars. The original locomotive saw little use after 1924 although it survived until recently behind the Laxey depot. For the centenary celebrations a replica was constructed, complete with its own bogies. It is seen here in Laxey station during one of the centenary event weeks. It was later converted to 3'0" gauge as a works car for the Manx Electric and numbered 34.

Below: The same wagon as illustrated earlier, this time with its sides attached and coupled to one of the trams in the station at Laxey. Behind is Manx Electric car No.9, decorated to advertise the forthcoming Steam 125 event of 1998.

Below: On the occasion of the evening running up the mountain, a large queue has gathered at Laxey wanting to experience the event. Car No.6 loads up while other trams are summoned from the depot to cope with the numbers.

While the Laxey depot was rebuilt, the trams were housed in this temporary shed constructed within the station area. On the occasion of the centenary year special stamp launch, one of the cars was required to operate to the summit with the stamps on board. Car No.2 was chosen for this duty and is seen here shortly before emerging for the day.

Later in the day the tram has returned to Laxey along with one of the later CAA railcars, that also went to the summit with the stamps. Note the snow on the front of the Railcar.

GREAT LAXEY MINES RAILWAY

Tramways of various kinds within the mining industry can be traced back many many years. Experience soon showed the mine operators that a wagon running on rails is moved far more easily than when not, whatever type of traction is employed.

The mines at Laxey, made famous by the vast Lady Isabella water-wheel, had several small tramways or railways running in the underground tunnels usually using human power. Two other lines served the mines, the Adit Tramway and the Glen Tramway, used to transfer the ore to the harbour for onward shipment and to bring materials for the mine back up from the harbour. It is the first of these two that dates back to 1823 that has now become what is known as the Great Laxey Mines Railway. Initially human power

was used, until April 1827 when a pony was purchased. The mine expanded and over the years so did the number of ponies, reaching five by 1846.

The line was extended to its current terminus in Valley Gardens in 1848 and in 1855 it was taken over by a private concern, who were paid 7d for each full wagon of ore moved from the mine. A few years later the mine company took the line back under their control.

The tramway continued to expand, 30 new wagons were purchased in 1873 and the number of ponies increased to nine. In the first six months of 1873 over 27,500 wagons of ore had been brought out of the mine.

A decision to replace the ponies with small steam locomotives was made in 1876. In order to determine the

Most of the route is surrounded by bushes and trees as illustrated by this view of one of the two locomotives out with an ore train and heading for the wheel end of the line.

Below: The restored line passes beneath the main Laxey to Ramsey road in a very small tunnel. Because of this tunnel the passenger vehicles have their entrance/exit on the outer end, thus providing the need for between the rails platforms. Here one of the platforms at the outer end of the line is illustrated while a train prepares for departure from the adjacent track. The footpath to the wheel is seen in the background.

Below:A view inside the original coach showing the unique design produced that allowed the line to start carrying passengers. The raised sections in the floor are where the wheels are.

The lines two sheds from the road above. The far one is the recently constructed carriage shed, while the locomotive shed is nearer the camera. Both locomotives are visible in this view, the older of the twp passenger vehicles has a good load of passengers.

Below: Ant arrives at Valley Gardens with an ore train during May 2006. There is now a junction outside the tunnel and passenger trains turn to the left of the picture into the new station.

Below: The method of entering and exiting the coach is clearly demonstrated here by volunteer Andrew Scarffe. The ten or so passengers will all have to exit in the same way. This design is required to allow a train to be evacuated in the tunnel if the need ever arose.

Tracklaying work underway at Valley Gardens to serve the new platforms is well advanced during the summer of 2007. The wheel sets in the background seem a little too wide?

A side on view of the same train identifies the locomotive as Ant with the original of the two passenger vehicles. It doesn't do for the driver to make too much smoke when travelling in this direction!

effects of the smoke from the locomotives in the mine, a number of small fires were lit. All was well so the locomotives were ordered and to accommodate their weight much of the track was relaid.

The locomotives were ordered from Stephen Lewin of Poole in Dorset and arrived together by Steamer on the 6th April 1877. Named Ant and Bee they had Works Nos. 684 and 685. These tiny machines were just 8'7" long, 3'0" wide and 4'9" high. They had solid 14" diameter wheels with wooden brake blocks on just the rear set of wheels. The driver stood within the rear frames, the two entering service in the mine during May 1877.

Various local modifications, probably mainly by the drivers, appeared on the locomotives over the years while their overall condition deteriorated to the extent that by 1905, their replacement was considered. Quotes were sought in early 1905 and Bagnall's, no doubt keen to penetrate the potential market for locomotives on the Island, even got as far as producing detailed drawings, these are dated May 1905.

Instead, probably due to the cost involved, it was decided to overhaul the existing locomotives. Interestingly Bagnall's got the contract to build the new boilers. In mid 1905 one of

the boilers was removed and shipped to Bagnall's workshops as a pattern. The first new boiler duly arrived, at a cost of £53.00, as was fitted before the second was removed. However, the project was a success and the second boiler was ordered and delivered by February 1906. One of the two also received a new chimney.

The ore from the mine was transported in chunky four-wheeled wagons, built on a cast-iron underframe, they were unsprung and unbraked and stood just 3'0" high. The bodies were hinged to the underframe to allow the ore to be tipped out on reaching the washing floors in Valley Gardens. Up to 200 wagons were in use in the mine at any one time and although some underframes were brought in, most of these wagons were built in the mines own workshops. Six or seven wagons usually made up a train.

Trains operated locomotive first into the mines and wagon first out to prevent the smoke blinding the driver on the outward trip. The person responsible for tipping the wagons usually rode in the last or first wagon.

Trains operated 16 hours a day, the crews working eight hours each starting at 06.00 and finishing at 22.00 with the changeover at 14.00. The early crew were required to start early enough to prepare the train and load any equipment required in the mine, in time for the first train in.

The tramway actually ran over the top of one of the shafts within the mine, requiring substantial timberwork to support the weight of a full train, while the line went round the top of most of the shafts.

Emerging from the actual mine, the line ran through a tunnel under the 'deads' and then through the tunnel under the main Laxey to Ramsey road and Manx Electric Railway, before emerging onto the upper level of the washing floors and terminating about where the current carriage shed is situated.

An ingenious uncoupling method using a chain across the boiler of the locomotive enabled the driver to uncouple the wagons without leaving his driving position.

The line continued to operate up to the end of the 1920s but, in early 1930 the little locomotives were locked away in their shed and left. Sadly in 1935 they were both broken up for scrap and the little line closed for good, or so it was thought!

Ant partially stripped down for repairs at the end of the 2008 season. The locomotive is being prepared for shipping away and even the nameplates have been removed, as has the dome cover.

A number of the original wagons used on the tramway survive and were brought to the surface by the Manx Mines Research Group in the early 1970s. Two are now on display at the Manx Museum and one at the mines yard at Laxey. Various examples of rails survive in use as fence posts, particularly in the area of the Machine House.

During the early 1980s, restoration of the line between the teams and adit was proposed by actor and one-time Laxey resident Michael Billington. The project failed following opposition from locals and the Manx Electricity Authority which had an electrical transformer in the tunnel at the start of the line.

In 1999 plans to restore a short length of the line were

announced by Laxey and Lonan Heritage Trust following the removal of the transformer. A donation from the estate of former Ramsey resident Lt Col Randolph Glen funded much of the infrastructure, and a replica engine shed was completed in 2003. More importantly, the estate also funded the construction of working replicas of both the Ant and Bee by Great Northern Steam Limited of Darlington, the replica Ant being delivered to the railway in April 2004. Six replica wagons had been completed by the Laxey blacksmith.

Work to build a concrete buttress to hold up the Manx Electric Railway and main road above the new GLMR station were completed, allowing work on the locomotive shed to be completed.

The new line was officially opened by the MHK for Garff, Mr Steve Rodan, on the 25th September 2004.

The western end of the line was extended to its new

A recent arrival on the line is this battery electric locomotive that has been christened Wasp. It is seen here at Valley Gardens station, connected to the charger between trips. The advantage of such traction to lines such as this, is the ability to switch on and go, rather than the lengthy and expensive process of raising steam.

terminus opposite the Laxey fire station for the 2005 season, making the total length of the line just over a quarter of a mile, while a revised track layout at the Glen Gardens end allowed easier shunting of the locomotives. The Lt Governor visited the line on Saturday the 6th August 2005.

Halloween trains were operated on the 22nd October, with the coach decorated with suitable spiders etc and the tunnel adorned with skeletons and witches painted onto boards attached to the tunnel sides. Ultraviolet lighting enhanced the spookiness.

A siding was added at the outer end of the line before Christmas 2005, adding flexibility in the operation of more than one train. Meanwhile plans to relay and move the Glen station to a site parallel with the main road had been drawn up.

The railway enjoyed a good season in 2006 with passenger numbers up on the previous year. Sunday the 20th August was of particular note with the official starting of the second Laxey Waterwheel in the adjacent Valley Gardens. The railway operated until 9.00pm that evening.

The Halloween trains were repeated, again with considerable numbers of passengers being carried.

The performance of 'Ant' one of the two locomotives had given rise to severe disappointment during 2006. Despite being less that three years old the locomotive was inspected at the end of the season and after a detailed report into its condition, it left the railway for the Alan Keefe works on the 13th January 2007.

A highly successful appeal was launched during 2006 to raise the funds needed to acquire a second passenger coach, an order being placed with Alan Keefe in February 2007.

Following planning approval for a new carriage shed and the relocation of the Valley Gardens Terminus, work on the new shed started in October 2006 and was completed in February 2007, the coach moved from its tunnel storage to the shed after tracklaying on the 10th March. The railway enjoyed a good summer season in 2007, with a number of special events bringing large numbers to the railway.

Following the completion of the new carriage shed, work continued on the new station in Valley Gardens, the two platform tracks and the new pointwork at the end of the tunnel being laid by the beginning of the 2007 season, although the joining curve was not completed. An extension to the siding at Mines Yard was also planned.

The Ant returned to the railway in July 2007 and has performed faultlessly ever since. Plans to send the Bee for similar treatment were made for when funds permit, hopefully over the 2008/09 winter. The second coach was delivered from Alan Keefe on the 8th August 2007. Seating nine or ten it has additional glazing behind the passenger seat, that as before runs lengthwise inside the coach. The existing coach was repainted over the 2007/08 winter having carried 21,000 passengers over the three seasons of operation..

The new Valley Gardens station was operational in time for the 2008 season and has been a useful addition to the railway. The railway continues to flourish, in particular events like the annual Halloween trains bringing in large numbers of passengers.

In May 2009 the first non-steam locomotive arrived on the line, allowing instant trains to operate if demand requires. Built by Clayton in 1973, the locomotive previously owned by a construction company, was refurbished by Alan Keefe before arriving on the Island. It carries the name Wasp, continuing the locomotive name theme.

Further general maintenance is being carried out over the current winter as preparations are made for 2010.

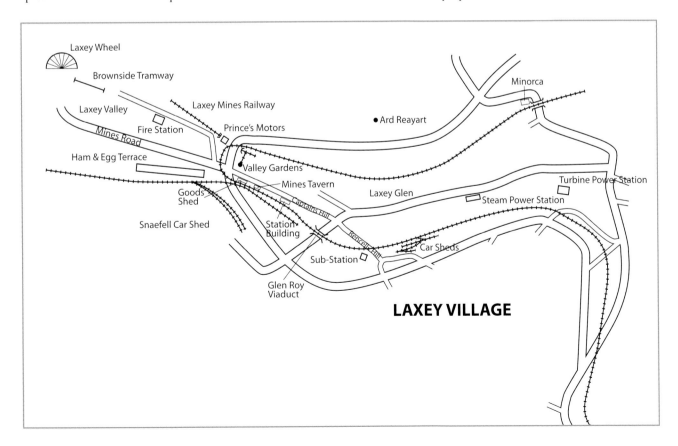

WILDLIFE PARK MINIATURE RAILWAY

The Manx Steam and Model Engineering Club was formed in 1985 by a group of enthusiasts who had built a number of 5" or 3½" gauge live steam locomotives. After several seasons travelling around the Island with a portable dual gauge track, the decision was taken to look for a site where a permanent miniature railway could be built. Negotiations with the Government resulted in an agreement to build and operate a three gauge (3½, 5 and 7¼") circular line within the Curraghs Wildlife Park.

Construction started in the late summer of 1991 and the railway, 'The Orchid Line', so named because of the wild orchids growing in the park, was officially opened by the Chief Minister in May 1992. At first the railway consisted of a single track circuit with a passing loop and a station. A steaming up area with a turntable was also constructed. The agreement with the Park Authority was to open the railway for the public every fortnight.

After two years of successful operation, the Club approached the Park Authority and agreement was reached to extend the railway from its initial 550ft length to around 1,750ft. This was carried out in two stages. The first stage in 1996 created an additional circuit round the outside of the original; the second stage was completed in 1997 by laying a third circuit, south of the original and 1996 extension, creating a figure of eight. At this stage the locomotive stock had increased with the addition of four 7¼" gauge locomotives. The 3½" gauge was and still is confined to the original circuit.

A 2006 view of the main station, known as Wagstaff Central, as diesel locomotive No.9 Violet Trescatheric passes on its first lap of the now substantial length line, with a good load of passengers clearly enjoying their trip.

Below: Some cruel person has taken Bobs ladder away, just as he was finishing off the roof of Wagstaff North signal box. There are a number of authentic buildings around the line, look out for them as you make your journey.

Below: One of the superb model locomotives that operate on the line. This LMS Crab is built to 7¼" gauge and carries the running number 2846. It is seen here taking on water at Wagstaff Central.

Diesel locomotive No.9 Violet Trescatheric departs from Wagstaff Central with a full train of excited passengers. The busy station area is visible behind.

Below: A little railway with a big atmosphere. A general view of Wagstaff Central with two trains awaiting departure for the journey around the park.

Below: The first section of the ride is the original part of the line, and takes the passengers once round the Ark. Here Sliecraeyder heads a four car train round the Ark on a bright sunny day in July 2008.

No miniature railway would be complete without at least one Great Western model. This super 7¼ model of Pannier tank No. 1366 rests in the preparation area of the line.

With its passengers getting a good view of the animals in the children's area, No.9 Violet Trescatheric is about to cross a road, as it nears the end of its journey round the park.

Sliecraeyder reaches the end of the Millennium section, has crossed the bridge and now crosses the road as it heads back onto the original section. There is still some way to go before journeys end.

A general view of the carriage shed and staff facility. The running line is on the far right.

7¼" gauge Schools class No. 30940 St Leonards, awaits departure from Wagstaff Central with a full train. The railway ticket office is visible to the right of the picture.

In 1999 the Club was given permission for a further extension of the line, bringing the total length to 3,042ft, by laying an extension through the wooded bog area called the Curragh, to the north of the original circle. The construction of this ambitious project was made possible by a grant received from the Mann 2000 Committee and a substantial private donation. The Millennium extension, as it has become known, opened in August 2000.

The railway is controlled by working signals throughout its length, the trains negotiating nine sets of points, two diamond crossings, five steel bridges and five level crossings, each controlled by authentic red flashing lights and buzzers. Each season, before operating commences, the track is inspected by a Government-appointed railway inspector. All the trains are fitted with vacuum brakes and carry a guard.

Since the 1992 season passenger numbers have steadily increased passing an annual total of 15,000 during 2003. The railway carried its 100,000th passenger in August 2004, the honour falling to Mr Robert Cannan of Wakefield who received a certificate and book token.

Two visiting locomotives for a weekend in August 2006 included a 5" gauge model of Loch. Despite these visits and a special Model Engineering weekend, passenger numbers for 2006 were sadly down by about 15% on 2005.

Just like the other railways on the Island, much of the track maintenance has to be carried out during the winter months. One of the bridges across to the bog section had its track and decking removed to allow access to the main steel structure for cleaning and painting during the 2006/07 winter. At the same time additional rolling stock was under construction to boost the capacity of the line for future seasons.

Despite the good start to 2007, the weather generally was poor but the line still managed to carry over 12,000 passengers.

Winter work for 2007/08 included the re-alignment of a 100 metre long curve to accommodate six coupled locomotives, two of which arrived on the railway for the 2008 season. During the recent winter the second bridge on the bog section of the railway has been refurbished.

The 2009 season produced good passenger numbers despite the generally awful weather. Further maintenance is planned for the current winter and the line looks forward to 2010 in anticipation of further success. Trains run every Sunday and Bank Holiday throughout the season and on Saturdays during the school summer holidays.

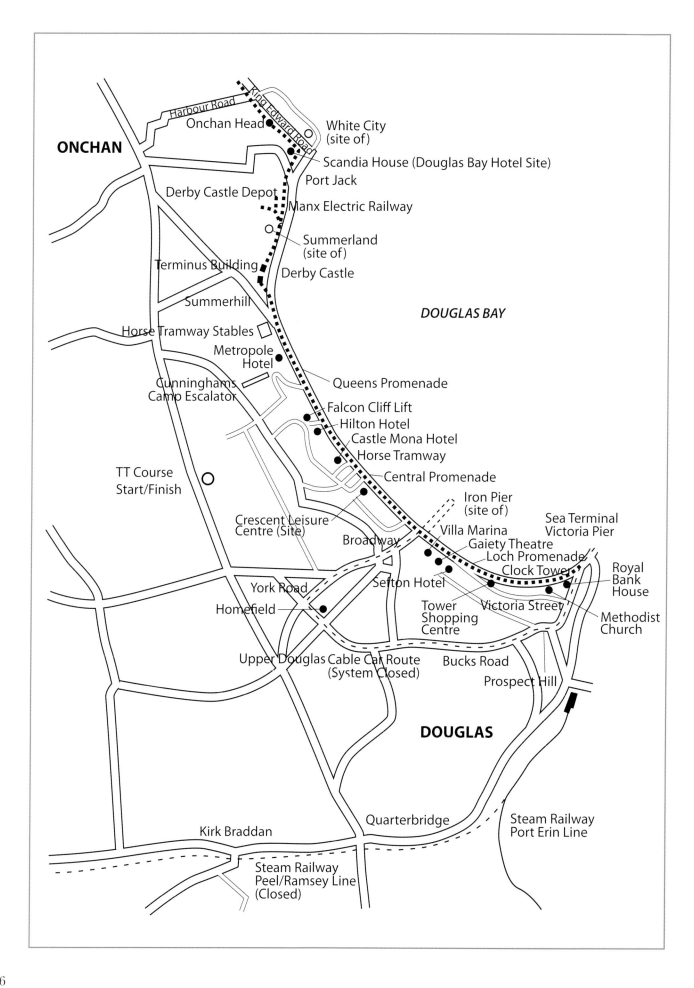

THE PORT SODERICK FUNICULAR

The Forrester family had developed Port Soderick bay into a major tourist attraction during the latter half of the 19th century. The arrival of the Douglas Southern Electric Tramway at the top of the cliff to the north of the bay in 1896 was an excellent boost to trade. The problem was the 150 steps between the tramway and bay!

In Douglas the Falcon Cliff Lift built in 1887 had ceased operating and so the Forrester's purchased the complete structure and had it re-erected at Port Soderick. New passenger cars were provided that were bigger than the original, the original ones surviving as kiosks at Port Soderick for many years.

The reconstructed line was longer than at Falcon Cliff and so some new sections had to be built but the basic structure of twin 4'0" gauge tracks of flat bottom rail was retained. Driven by an oil engine the cables were of 3½" circumference. The building at the top of the line was of corrugated iron, the lower sections of the line, essentially a wooden structure, was raised on stone pillars which are still visible today.

Inspected and approved on the 9th July 1898, the final approval to begin carrying passengers came in a letter from the Governors secretary dated the 11th July 1898.

It is not clear how long the line survived, its seems likely however that it closed around the same time as the Marine Drive tramway in 1939.

The whole complex at Port Soderick was sold in 1947 and the lift ceased operating. It was dismantled by 1949, the cars surviving as hen houses until a few cattle were poisoned by chewing the lead paint on the roofs.

There are many pictures of the Port Soderick Funicular Railway, mostly in views taken from the other side of the bay and therefore making the views somewhat distant. This superb picture has come to light recently. The structure supported on stone pillars is shown to advantage complete with its advertising up the side of the track base. The picture also shows how far away the terminus of the Marine Drive Tramway was from the top of the funicular, the wooden nameboard-like structure to the right of the picture marking that terminus. (Tony Wilson Collection)

DOUGLAS HEAD AND MARINE DRIVE TRAMWAY

Douglas Head had, by the 1880s, become a popular spot and several schemes to develop it further were contemplated. These included a tunnel under the harbour with a spiral staircase, a suspension bridge over the harbour and even a tramway up from South Quay.

In the early 1890s a scenic road was promoted along to Port Soderick but various difficulties slowed the construction. However, by the 7th August 1893 it had reached Little Ness and a celebration function was held, at which it was announced that an electric tramway would be constructed along the route.

Douglas Southern Electric Tramways Ltd was incorporated on the 21st October 1895 to build and own a

building of the road had involved a number of bridges constructed of timber. These were replaced by steel structures to accommodate the tramway. Unlike all the other railways on the Island, the tramway was built to the British Standard gauge of 4'8½".

On Thursday the 16th July, with completion of the tramway as far as Keristal, an opening ceremony was held. Three special cars conveyed invited guests along the

Another of the bridges was at Pigeon's Stream where the line's power station was also built. This picture taken some while after the line closed shows the power station building to advantage despite the holes in the roof. (Tony Wilson Collection)

The line was well known for its spectacular viaducts, that at Wallberry being no exception. Had the tramway survived it would now represent a wonderful tourist attraction, travelling as it did along a superb stretch of coastline. (Tony Wilson Collection)

new tramway from Douglas Head to Little Ness with a later extension to Port Soderick and a possible branch to join up with the Old Castletown Road near Oakhill.

Construction of the tramway started at the beginning of 1896 and by late February the trackbed was almost completed and the track had arrived. A car shed was built at Little Ness and a power station at Pigeon Stream. The

completed section despite no inspections having been carried out. The various inspections followed the opening and after a few adjustments the line opened to the public on the 7th August 1896. That season ended on the 26th September with 53,536 passengers having travelled on the trams over the course of that season.

Construction of the remainder of the tramway was undertaken over the 1896/97 winter and the complete line opened to the public on the first day of the 1897 season, the 1st April. A journey along the line, high above the sea and

Car No.7 is captured at the Douglas Head terminus showing one of the round number disks hanging on the front end. That number shows '5' indicating that at the time this picture was taken a five-tram service was in operation. The positioning of the overhead trolley pole to the side of the tram is clearly shown as are the ornate overhead poles. (Tony Wilson Collection)

with the cliff face climbing high above the tram on the landward side and some warm sunshine, must have been a super experience.

At peak times a 7½ minute interval service was provided and a clever system to prevent accidents was employed. On the overhead poles at the passing loops, numbers were painted representing the number of cars in service. If a seven car service was operating they should pass at loops marked with a seven, five car services passed at loops marked five and so on.

Services were curtailed at the outbreak of war in August 1914 and for around four years the line was silent. In early 1919 preparations begun for a reopening of the line and 1920 provided one of the best operating seasons ever. Passenger numbers declined through the 1920s and by 1929 despite 101,600 passengers, the tramway made a loss of £94.

Like the other railways on the Island the line was having to compete with motor bus services and excursions, and itself tried to get consent to operate a charabanc service from the town centre up to the head to boost traffic on the tramway, but this application was unsuccessful.

Fares were reduced for 1936 and electric headlights were

fitted to the cars to allow late evening trips in a bid to increase passenger numbers.

In the event, nothing seemed to bring passengers in sufficient numbers and the line operated for the final time on Wednesday the 15th September 1939.

Track and overhead was removed in 1946/47 but, the depot and its contents remained untouched until in 1951 a group led by Keith Pearson acquired and removed car No.1 from the shed, hauled it along the narrow Marine Drive and into preservation. It was intended to return and claim a second car but this was not possible. The remainder of the cars and the shed were demolished over the 1951/52 winter.

The preserved tram is now restored and on display at the Crich Tramway Museum in Derbyshire.

DOUGLAS HEAD INCLINE RAILWAY

The story of this 450ft long 4'0" gauge railway begun on the 21st January 1898. An agreement between Sir John Goldie-Taubman and R. M. Broadbent, allowed for a single or double-track mechanical tramway, lift or railway and lift, from a point near Battery Pier to a point seaward of the Douglas Southern Electric Tramway terminus on Douglas Head. Richard Broadbent and his wife had formed Douglas Head Incline Railway Company Ltd with a capital of £10,000.

The line was built in 1900 and consisted of a double-track funicular railway climbing at a gradient of 1 in 4.5. The lower station was behind the Douglas Head Lighthouse near Port Skillion while the upper end had a combined station and engine house not far from the Douglas Southern terminus. There was a curve about one-third of the way up and the track was laid with 70lb flat bottom rail.

Two stepped cars were delivered from Hurst Nelson & Co. of Motherwell in July 1900 (drawing numbers 5072 & 5025) and the line is thought to have opened later that year.

The entire undertaking was sold to Douglas Head Incline Railway Ltd on the 7th July 1922, the new company having its offices at the upper station. A Nunnery estate deed of the 30th June 1926 required the line to operate from the Friday before Whitsun Monday until the 30th September each year. It was closed during both world wars.

The service was restarted in 1949 but the whole line was disused by 1954 having outlasted the ferry service that connected the two piers in the harbour. There is some thought that the line changed hands in 1940 and again in 1947.

Whichever company owned the line by 1954 was liquidated that year, the line itself was dismantled in October and November 1955 and the winding up came on the 15th October 1956. Some of the rail was reused on the Manx Electric on the outskirts of Ramsey.

A wonderful view of the Douglas Head area with a railway car clearly visible to the left of the picture, passing a point where there was a substantial retaining wall for the railway. A vast array of Steam Packet and other vessels will be keeping the Harbour Master busy. (Tony Wilson Collection)

UPPER DOUGLAS CABLE TRAMWAY

At a public meeting on the 19th January 1894 the residents of Upper Douglas pressed for a proper tram service to the area as they felt that the lack of such a service, in comparison to the Promenade, was having a detrimental effect on the shops and boarding houses in Upper Douglas.

The Upper Douglas Tramway Committee met for the first time on the 9th April 1894 and a later meeting of the Commissioners, now Corporation, Improvement Committee resolved that it would be desirable to construct a tramway to the Upper Douglas area.

The proposed route was from the bottom of Victoria Street to the bottom of Broadway near its junction with the Promenade. The cost of an electric line would be around £19,000 while a cable tramway would be around £25,000.

Little progress resulted in a further public meeting on the 21st January 1895 to try and push the project forward. Meanwhile, there we ongoing negotiations between the Commissioners and the Isle of Man Tramways & Electric Power Co. over the Horse Tramway and the Tramway Company offered to build the new line as part of the deal. A formal offer was made on the 30th May 1895.

The Commissioners decided to accept this proposal and promoted a bill to Tynwald, this becoming the Upper Douglas Tramway Act 1895. Standing Orders were suspended in the house on the 10th July to allow a special committee to debate the application urgently.

The act was passed on the 3rd August 1895 specifying a tramway operated by wire, ropes, cables or chains with a fixed engine, starting at the junction of Victoria Street and the Promenade, travelling up Victoria Street, Prospect Hill, Bucks Road, Woodbourne Road, York Road Ballaquayle Road and terminating at the bottom of Broadway adjacent to its junction with the Promenades, thus connecting with the Horse Tramway at both ends. The track gauge was specified

The preserved cable tram carries two different numbers, 72 and 73, because it was made up from the remains of the two trams. Here we see car No.73 in service in Woodbourne Road just short of what is now its junction with York Road at the turn of the century. Notice the complete lack of buildings beyond the tram looking towards what is now Nobles Park.

Cable tram No.77 is seen in York Road in the early years of the 20th Century, before it was rebuilt to a saloon vehicle. This in this form is one of the sister cars to the preserved example. The roof board advertises other local attractions including the Snaefell Mountain Railway.

as 3'0". From here a continuous cable of some three miles in length drove the tramway, the individual cars gripping on to it when they needed to move.

Despite some concerns from local traders about the proximity of moving trams to their property, construction of the line started. Further problems brought construction to a halt in February 1896 but this too was soon resolved. A car shed and engine house was constructed on a site off York Road between Laureston Avenue and Waverley Road.

The cable was threaded on the 6th and 7th August 1896 using two traction engines, the first tramcar actually venturing out onto the line late on Friday the 7th August 1896. Following testing and inspections the tramway opened to the public on Saturday the 15th August 1896, three cars providing a ten-minute service. The line carried 193,645 passengers between opening and the end of the year.

In February 1900 Dumbell's Bank collapsed taking with it many companies including the IOMT&EP Co. Eventually after various reports and inspections the Corporation, as they were by then known, offered £40,000 for both the horse and cable tramways, this was rejected but a later offer of £50,000 was accepted on the 25th September 1901.

The line was shortened in 1902 to terminate just below the depot on Ballaquayle Road.

The tramway continued to operate with good passenger numbers, including through the First World War when a reduced service was provided. The Corporation, concerned about the condition of the tramway and the costs of repairs, ordered five Tilling Stevens petrol electric buses in 1920 and these took over the tramway route for the 1921/22 winter.

Thereafter the tramway only operated during the summer season, each year for a shorter period than the last until eventually in 1929 it ran only for a few weeks.

Sadly the end had come and the last cars ran on Monday the 19th August 1929, the press reporting Douglas to be 'strangely quiet on the Tuesday', without the clanking noise of the trams. The cable was soon removed and the removal of trackwork started. The depot was converted to a bus garage for the corporation and survived into National Transport days, the site is now a sheltered housing complex.

The cars were all sold to one local businessman who intended to sell them on as holiday bungalows, two did find their way to use as a dwelling in the north of the Island, while the rest were broken up.

The two survivors did just that and were eventually rescued by the Douglas Cable Car Group and moved to space loaned to the Group in the former depot in York Road where over an eight-year period the two were made into one and a fully restored car took part in the centenary celebration cavalcade for the Horse Tramway in August 1976. The car is now on display in the Horse Tramway depot at Derby Castle although it is hoped that it will soon move to the newly created Transport Museum at Jurby.

The tramway returned to the news in January 2000 when excavations in connection with the Island-wide IRIS scheme unearthed two of the original Cable wheels at the bottom of Victoria Street. Efforts by local enthusiasts and the engineering firm employed on the contract, allowed one of the wheels to be retrieved intact and this will be joining the restored car at Jurby.

CHAPTER THIRTEEN

THE FALCON CLIFF LIFT

The Falcon Cliff Hotel, now office accommodation, was developed in the 1880s as an entertainment complex, which from its prominent position commands superb views over Douglas Bay.

A cliff lift was built in 1887 to carry visitors up from the Promenades to the complex. This lift was a 'Patent Tram' lift built by T. Cain and was first tested on the 26th May 1887. It was 218ft long and rose to a point 110ft above the Promenade. It was a double track 4'0" gauge line with flat bottom rail fastened to 12" square timbers that formed the top of a viaduct-like construction up the cliff side.

The lift was inspected by the Harbour Commissioners in July and the forthcoming opening was announced. However, the line did not actually start operating until the 6th August 1887. It is not clear whether this lift was powered by Steam, Oil or Gas. The journey time was 1min 25seconds.

The lift was out of use by 1896 and was sold to the Forrester Family, dismantled and later installed at Port Soderick.

Thirty-one years later a new lift was built up to the complex, this time though just a single-track line built on a new site to the left of the original line. W. M. Wadsworth of

A view of the Falcon Cliff lift from the top station showing the single car during its journey. The unusual arrangement of overhead wires and contacts mounted on top of the car is clearly visible. (Tony Wilson Collection)

Bolton were the engineers, the new line being of 5'0" gauge running in channel section rails set at an angle of 45 degrees. A balance weight (weight of car plus half load of six passengers) runs up and down in its own guides under the car.

When built, this new line was operated by a 400 volt DC electric motor driving twin 1" diameter cables, when DC supply was ceased in Douglas a rectifier was installed on the site and electricity was delivered at 415 volts in three phase.

Initially the line operated all year round but in latter years it was only seasonal.

Latterly owned by Okells Brewery in Douglas, the decline in tourism in the 1980s led to the closure of the complex and hence the lift in 1989. Although still in situ the lift has not operated in service since then.

There are plans to move the lift to Groudle Glen to improve access to the Groudle Glen Railway.

A somewhat unusual view of the lift, this time from near the lower station. The car is either about to or has already passed the counterweight seen lower than the car and running on the lower face of the angle rails that also support the actual passenger car. The steps to the right of the picture provide a more energetic way of reaching the top. (Tony Wilson Collection)

CHAPTER FOURTEEN

THE CUNNINGHAM CAMP ESCALATOR

The Camp – A Brief History

Joseph Cunningham was a Liverpool Scot who moved to the Isle of Man in 1884. After getting married, he and his wife lived at Oirr Ushtey on the Promenade in Laxey from where they provided all the meals to their very first campers. In these early days the accommodation was in tents alongside the river.

The Cunninghams moved to what became Howstrake Camp in 1887 and 32 years later moved again, this time to Victoria Road and what became Cunningham's Young Men's Holiday Camp.

Joseph Cunningham died in 1924 but the camp continued to flourish with an average annual attendance during the 1930s of 36,000 campers.

The camp was later renamed Douglas Holiday Camp and eventually Isle of Man Holiday Centre.

The Patent

On the 24th August 1908 Archibald Laidlaw Baird of 5 and 6 Clements Inn, London, WC2, provisionally applied for a patent, the actual application coming on the 24th March 1909. The application had been communicated from Joseph O. Boufard of 108 Dearborn Street, Chicago, USA.

The application noted: 'This invention relates to improvements in escalators or inclined elevators of that type in which seats are fitted at intervals to an endless driving chain.'

The patent was accepted on the 3rd June 1909 and given UK Patent number 17757.

Planning Applications

The various planning applications would indicate that plans for the escalator began before the First World War. This is suggested by the application to build the new entrance in Switzerland Road as early as 1914. While there was a stone gravel path up to the camp from this entrance, it may well be that this was an afterthought, when it became clear that the escalator could not be completed before the end of hostilities.

Plans for the actual escalator were not submitted until the 13th January 1923 No.1793, they were approved by the

A little way up Switzerland Road in Douglas is this wonderful stone-built entrance, now sadly bricked up. Thought to date from the 1940s this view shows the escalator structure climbing up to the left of the picture and visible through the arch is a large 'Escalator' sign. Although described as an escalator it was nothing like the machine we today know by that name.

Highways Committee later that month and by Douglas Council on the 14th February 1923. This original escalator is the left hand one, when seen from the bottom.

A letter from architects Geo Kay & Sons of Douglas, dated the 13th January 1923, indicates that the design was not theirs, but had been traced from the engineers drawings 'who had put up a many of these'.

The second escalator was the subject of application No.3849 on the 3rd July 1937, was approved by the Works Committee on the 10th August 1937 and by Full Council on the 8th September 1937. Work started on the 15th November and was completed on the 27th June 1938, the architect was J. E. Teare.

Construction of the Escalator

Following the passing of planning permission, work on the construction of the escalator started without delay. It is known that the drawings produced by Geo Kay & Sons were traced from the engineering company drawings but who those were produced by remains a mystery.

It seems likely that two different contractors were involved in the actual construction, one for the mechanics and another for the wooden structure. As both the entrance in Switzerland Road and the 1937 extension to the escalator were built by J. Skillicorn of Onchan, it seems reasonable that they were also responsible for the original wooden structure but this is yet to be established.

Possible contractors and or designers of the mechanical side of the machine could be one of any number of companies but, likely candidates are:

H. Breakell & Co. Ltd of Chorley, Lancashire; Etchells, Congdon & Muir of Manchester; W. M. Wadsworth Lifts & Co. Ltd of Bolton; T. Cain; Jack Morgan of Croydon Surrey.

The gearbox on the original installation was supplied by Crofts Engineers of Bradford and has serial number 85737, the specification plate quoting an operating power of 12.5hp at 360rpm.

One point against the Wadsworth possibility is that with the original drawings for the Falcon Cliff Lift held by Douglas Corporation are copies of Wadsworth drawings, whereas no such copies are with the original drawings for the escalator.

There are also some notes in a letter that indicate that the Cunningham's own engineers workshops were involved in drilling and cutting parts for the escalator, so it is possible

One picture of the escalator in use does exist in another publication but, no original copy has been found. This view inside the newer of the two installations was taken after closure. Each passenger sat sideways to the direction of travel in an individual seat, each made up of eight different sections of wood. There were 100 seats on each installation.

that it was built 'in house'.

Whoever built it, the escalator was a considerable success and in July 1937 an application was lodged with Douglas Council for an extension to the building to allow a second set of seats to be installed to the right of the existing set when looking from the bottom.

Work on the extension started on the 15th November 1937 and was completed by the 27th June. J. Skillicorn were the builders of at least the wooden structure. The motor for the second set was provided by British Thompson Houston of Rugby (now Alstom PLC). It was a 415 volt induction motor serial No. 471145-1-01 with frame No. 6329GK and delivered 20bhp when running at 586rpm.

Each individual set of seats comprises 100 chairs, 48 of which are visible; the remaining 52 are making their way

back to the bottom underneath and upside down. Adjacent to each set of seats was a 170 step staircase.

Only the left hand, indeed the original, survived in service to the end, indeed it would appear that the newer set did not operate after the 1964 season.

Operation of the Escalator

Campers originally rode on the escalator free of charge but other members of the public were charged 1d. This charge did rise very slowly over the years and by the time the escalator closed in 1968 it had reached 3d!

The escalator ran throughout the season from May

A recent picture of the older installation following the collapse of the outer retaining wall. It clearly shows the seats 'Returning' to the bottom underneath those that would have been occupied that are visible towards the top of the picture. The newer set are also just visible. The vast amounts of timber used in the construction are clear from this view. It will not be long before this whole structure collapses and this unique example of early escalator technology will be lost forever.

through to September from early morning to late evening. Actual times vary from source to source but appear to be from 6.00 or 6.30 am until 11.30 or 11.45 pm. Campers returning after midnight who were caught had to walk up and were fined 1 shilling. The first passenger on the escalator is believed to have been a Mr Tinker from Middleton in Manchester.

From 1938 onwards there was a small ticket office on the right-hand side of the entrance at the bottom.

The chairs were driven electrically as discussed earlier, the motor running continuously with a clutch at the top that could be used to stop the escalator if necessary. There is evidence of some sort of physical bell communication between the attendants at the top and bottom of the installation.

The motor installations for both sets were housed in a concrete building under the top platform of the structure.

There are indications that the whole thing ran on 110 volts until early 1964 when the voltage was increased but, the motor that remains in situ on the newer side shows three phase 415 volts.

There was a start lever at the bottom and a safety bar at the top, that presumably stopped the seats moving if a passenger failed to get off at the top.

The Southend Connection

Previous research into the history of the Cunningham's installation have indicated a link with a similar machine in Southend-on-Sea.

Following this apparent lead, a considerable amount of research has been undertaken about the Southend machine. The conclusion is that it is possible that a number of parts, possibly items such as motors and gearboxes were sold to Cunningham's but, the actual installation type was completely different and so was certainly not simply dismantled from Southend and re-erected in Douglas.

The Southend installation was built by the Reno Inclined Elevator Construction Syndicate in 1901 and was certainly one of the very first such elevators constructed in Britain. The very first public escalator for everyday use in the UK was at Seaforth Sands station on the Liverpool Overhead Railway and was similar in style to that at Southend.

In common with Cunningham's, the Southend one was installed inside a long wooden shed and opened on the 3rd September 1901 and by the 10th September had transported 34,853 passengers, providing a net profit for the operator of £87 4s 6d. At this time the Reno Company was in negotiations to build similar machines at Clacton-on-Sea, Ramsgate and Tynemouth.

It was a moving walkway consisting of an endless wooden-slatted conveyor on a chain angled at 20 to 25 degrees (1 in 5) or slightly steeper, and was found to be uncomfortable for passengers to stand on. It was powered by a 35hp electric motor and was capable of carrying 3,000 passengers per hour.

Many complaints were received about the noise and there were frequent mechanical breakdowns, leading to closure in 1912, and later the whole thing being dismantled and stored.

The 1912 dismantling fits with the apparent intentions of Cunninghams, indicated by the entrance construction in 1914. It is therefore possible that the Southend equipment was sold to Cunninghams almost immediately after dismantling and stored on the Island until used in the construction in 1923.

Another important link between Southend and Douglas and perhaps the most likely to have influenced the purchase of the Southend equipment for Cunninghams was one Bertram Kelly.

Born in Douglas the son of Captain James Kelly, the family left the Island around 1887 to allow Captain Kelly to take up the position of Manager, Southend-on-Sea Pier, Pavilion and Electric Tramways. Bertram Kelly later held positions in Electrical and Lighting engineering with Hornsea Borough Council, London County Council and the Midland Railway before returning to the Island and the Manx Electric Railway. In September 1922 he became the first electrical engineer for the Borough of Douglas.

One other interesting similarity between the two is in relation to noise. There were many complaints in Southend about the noise and it is said that the Douglas sets were also noisy. Indeed the owners of one of the adjacent properties at the top of the Douglas installation have in their deeds that they are not allowed to complain about the noise created by the escalator. There is also a story that if the wind was right it could be heard in Liverpool!

Personnel

During the vast amounts of research to try and trace the origin of this installation, a number of names of people involved with the escalator over the years have been discovered:

Maurice Kennaugh, worked as an apprentice electrician around 1964; Cliffy Kane, a camp handyman who worked on the escalator at some time; Eric Callow, the last senior electrician at the camp; Richard Stevenson, a former operator of the escalator; Alan Cojeen, an employee of the camp for 25 years; Colin Goldsmith, one of the last escalator operators.

Its Place in History

The Cunningham's Escalator was built at a time when escalator technology was advancing rapidly and names such as Otis were beginning to appear on the scene. Jessie Reno whose name appears on many early patents, produced the early versions of what was installed at Cunningham's. The patent referred to earlier in these notes was simply an improvement or modification to those basic designs.

While it cannot be stated as fact, no evidence of any other similar structure or mechanism has been uncovered, and so it seems likely that the Douglas escalator is unique and will now remain so.

The camp itself was the beginnings of establishments such as Butlins and had within its boundary a fabulous example of early escalator technology, the forerunner to a piece of everyday life today.

THE BROWSIDE TRAMWAY

The Browside Tramway was a short passenger-carrying line serving the Laxey Wheel. It was built and indeed operated by Captain Reddicliffe, John Callow who was the Mining Company Clerk and John Corlett the Captain of the North Laxey Mine. It opened on the 16th August 1890.

It was a simple funicular railway, 130 yards long with a track gauge of 6'0", the two tracks being about three feet apart. It was worked by water, in similar fashion to others around the world. The two cars had water tanks underneath; the car at the top having its tank filled while the one at the bottom had its emptied. When the brake was released the extra weight of the upper car was sufficient to move both cars. On arrival at the other end of the line the car now at the bottom had its tank emptied and the one at the top filled and the process began again. The tramway paid the Mining Company a rent of £25 per year for the water it used.

The cars seated around 50 passengers on eight toastrack-style seats and were completely open.

A small accident occurred in 1893 when the brake was not applied properly and the cars ran away, one slamming into the bottom station: the other into the top and jamming itself. No injuries were suffered by passengers but, Mr Callow who happened to be at the top station did receive minor injuries after being hit by the ascending car.

The fare charged seemed to vary, some sources state a 1d return, some a 1d each way and indeed one suggestion is 1d up and ½d down.

The line employed a bung boy at the lower station whose job it was to empty the tank of the car that had just completed the descent.

In January 1905 the rent for 1904 had not been paid and negotiations with the Mining Company got the rent reduced for the forthcoming season to £15. The owners did offer the Mining Company a share in the line but this was rejected.

At the beginning of 1906, the Mining Company increased the rent to £50 for the approaching season, eventually an agreement was reached for a payment of £25. The year of 1906 is thought to have been the last season of operation, the line was sold to a Robert Kelly of Douglas, he in turn receiving a letter from the Mining Company saying that they could no longer supply water to operate the tramway because they did not have enough!

The line had been dismantled by 1910, the remains of the upper station disappearing under the new car park at the wheel. Mention was made in the mid 1970s by Laxey Village commissioners of restoring the line but nothing has ever come of this idea.

A view from the upper station showing one of the passenger cars and what would appear to be an intermediate station although there does not appear to be a similar platform on the other side. The bottom station is visible beyond what is almost a cutting formed by the trees.

CHAPTER SIXTEEN

RAMSEY PIER TRAMWAY

The 2,160 ft (658.4m) long Ramsey Pier was built by Messrs. Head, Wrighton & Sons of Stockton-on-Tees at a cost of £45,000. It was opened by the Lord Bishop of Sodor and Man on the 22nd July 1886.

Some documentation indicates that the tramway was built at the same time as the pier and indeed used during the construction to convey materials, while some indicate that it was added later. An order dated 1895 for rails to lay the tramway would seem to indicate that it was added later. It seems unlikely that the rails needed replacing after such a short time, and a mid 1890s picture shows the pier minus tramway.

The line is 2,080ft (634.0m) long with a central passing loop, a short siding at both ends and at the shore end two divided spurs stretched off the pier onto the road. These were removed in 1955/56. It is 3'0" (0.92m) gauge and is laid with 45lb tramway type grooved rail.

The original rolling stock consisted of seven luggage trucks and one low flat truck all dating from either 1886 or 1899. The ninth item was added in 1899 and was a passenger-carrying hand-propelled vehicle with upholstered seats for around six.

Modernisation came in 1937 with the addition of a Planet locomotive and four-wheeled 15-seat passenger coach, both from F. C. Hibberd & Co. of Park Royal, London, the 8hp

An early colour view of the Planet locomotive and coach at the outer end of the pier alongside one of the luggage trucks. Sadly the building and the crane have now disappeared, one of the luggage trucks survives on the pier and the Planet and coach are in private preservation. (Tony Wilson Collection)

locomotive having works number 2037 and the coach 2038.

In 1950 a Wickham railcar, works No.5763, with Ford V8 engine and seating for 11 passengers arrived. Two members of the Royal Family have travelled on the line, Edward VII and Queen Elizabeth the Queen Mother on the 4th July 1963, the Planet locomotive and coach doing the honours on this occasion.

The line operated until the 9th September 1981 when it was closed following the discovery that the wooden track bearers needed replacement. In its final season the line carried 7,000 passengers and completed 900 operational miles.

The Planet locomotive and the Wickham were used in the dismantling of the former Manx Northern railway from St. John's to Ramsey. The Wickham was dismantled in 1983, the Planet and coach are preserved by the Isle of Man Railway & Tramway Preservation Society and currently reside in the Manx Electric car shed at Ramsey.

The Pier still stands although closed to public access, the story of its survival or not needing a book of its own. However, as we go to press it does seem that the Pier will be preserved and therefore that one day the Planet and coach may return to their rightful home. We will just have to wait and see.

The 1950 Wickam railcar is seen at the mid-way passing loop, the prices quoted in decimal pence dating this view to post 1971. This railcar later saw service on the Steam Railway but has now been broken up. (Tony Wilson Collection)

CHAPTER SEVENTEEN

THE KNOCKALOE BRANCH

At the outbreak of the first World War the Isle of Man Railway Company was called upon by the British Government to build and operate a rail link between Peel and a new internment camp at Knockaloe. The cost was met entirely by the British Government. Knockaloe was already an established seasonal army camp and was selected as being the most suitable site for the detention camp, the site opening as such on the 17th November 1914.

The new branch left the main Peel to Douglas line about 200 yards east of Glenfaba Mill and opened just under a year after the actual camp, on the 1st September 1915. The purpose of the new railway was to carry supplies of fuel, food, general stores and of course, the prisoners and prison guards to the camp, and remove rubbish from the camp for disposal in Peel. Some of the 'rubbish' was however retained by the prisoners, large meat bones for instance were carved into figures for sale, many of these figures survive today and are collectively known as "Knockaloe Ware" and can attract high prices if and when they become available.

The junction with the Isle of Man Railway was controlled by a patent 'Annett Key' which locked the pointwork and when the line was lifted this key was transferred to Poortown

and used for the quarry siding. The branch curved sharply south over the River Neb climbing at a remarkable 1 in 20 gradient. On the curve between the junction and the Neb Bridge there was a passing loop, where the train engine ran round the train, in order to push it up the gradient, pushing was preferred to pulling for obvious safety reasons! The line then continued across a field along the east side of the main Patrick Road until turning sharply just before Patrick Church, crossing the road and entering the camp itself. It kept to the left-hand side of the main drive to its terminus at the camp headquarters.

Locomotive No.15 Caledonia was usually used on the branch as it was, and still is, the largest and most powerful locomotive, in the fleet. It was intended to keep the locomotive in a shed at Knockaloe but the chimney was too high to enter the shed, so the first two roof joists were sawn off enabling the engine to gain access! In reality it would seem that the loco returned to Peel most of the time and was left out in the open, the crew probably thought it a better idea to ride back to Peel rather than walk!

Following the end of hostilities, the line closed on the 4th October 1920 and the track was lifted during 1923/24.

Pictures of the Knockaloe Prisoner of War Camp in the village of Patrick are few and far between. However, this super picture does exist and is worthy of inclusion here despite having been published before. It shows Isle of Man Railway No.15 Caledonia within the confines of the camp. Just about visible at the far end of the locomotive are a couple of wagons, no doubt bringing supplies to the camp. The Camp Guards to the right of the entrance seem to be deliberately ignoring the photographer! The wooden huts have long gone but, the stone-walled entrance still survives and today provides the entrance to the Isle of Man Government farm.

FLEET LIST

These lists include all items of rolling stock that still survive, although not all still reside on the Island.

MANX ELECTRIC RAILWAY POWER CARS (3'0" Gauge)

No.	Built by	Year	Bogies	Motors	Car Type	No. of seats	Length	Width	Height	Notes
1	Milnes	1893	Milnes S3	2 x 25hp	Unvestibuled saloon	34	34'9" 10.59m	6'6" 1.98m	11'0" 3.35m	In service
2	Milnes	1893	Milnes S3	2 x 25hp	Unvestibuled saloon	34	34'9" 10.59m	6'6" 1.98m	11'0" 3.35m	In service
5	Milnes	1894	Milnes S3	2 x 25hp	Vestibuled saloon	32	34'8" 10.56m	6'3" 1.90m	11'0" 3.35m	In service
6	Milnes	1894	Milnes S3	2 x 25hp	Vestibuled saloon	36	34'8" 10.56m	6'3" 1.90m	11'0" 3.35m	In service
7	Milnes	1894	Milnes S3	2 x 25hp	Vestibuled Saloon	36	34'8" 10.56m	6'3" 1.90m	11'0" 3.35m	In service
9	Milnes	1894	Milnes S3	2 x 25hp	Vestibuled saloon	36	34'8" 10.56m	6'3" 1.90m	11'0" 3.35m	In service Illuminated Car
14	Milnes	1898	Milnes S3	4 x 20hp	Cross bench open	56	35'5" 10.79m	6'3" 1.90m	10'6" 3.20m	Stored
15	Milnes	1898	Milnes S3	4 x 20hp	Cross bench open	56	35'5" 10.79m	6'3" 1.90m	10'6" 3.20m	Stored
16	Milnes	1898	Milnes S3	4 x 20hp	Cross bench open	56	35'5" 10.79m	6'3" 1.90m	10'6" 3.20m	In service
17	Milnes	1898	Milnes S3	4 x 20hp	Cross bench open	56	35'5" 10.79m	6'3" 1.90m	10'6" 3.20m	Stored
18	Milnes	1898	Milnes S3	4 x 20hp	Cross bench open	56	35'5" 10.79m	6'3" 1.90m	10'6" 3.20m	Stored
19	Milnes	1899	Milnes S3	4 x 20hp	Winter saloon	48	37'6" 11.43m	7'4" 2.23m	11'0" 3.35m	In service
20	Milnes	1899	Milnes S3	4 x 20hp	Winter saloon	48	37'6" 11.43m	7'4" 2.23m	11'0" 3.35m	In service
21	Milnes	1899	Milnes S3	4 x 20hp	Winter saloon	48	37'6" 11.43m	7'4" 2.23m	11'0" 3.35m	In service
22	McArds (Port Erin)	1992	Brill 27Cx	4 x 25hp	Winter saloon	48	37'6" 11.43m	7'4" 2.23m	11'0" 3.35m	Replacement In service
23	MER Co. Ltd	1926	(Brill 27Cx)	(4 x 27.5hp)	Locomotive	—	34'6" 10.51m	6'3" 1.90m	10'0" 3.04m	Stored
25	Milnes MER	1898	Brush Type D		Cross bench open	56	35'5" 10.79m	6'3" 1.90m	10'6" 3.20m	Stored
26	Milnes /MER	1898	Brush Type D		Cross bench open	56	35'5" 10.79m	6'3" 1.90m	10'6" 3.20m	In service
27	Milnes /MER	1898	Brush Type D		Cross bench open	56	35'5" 10.79m	6'3" 1.90m	10'6" 3.20m	Stored
28	ER&TCW Ltd	1904	Brill 27Cx	4 x 25hp	Cross bench open	56	35'0" 10.66m	6'3" 1.90m	10'6" 3.20m	Stored
29	ER&TCW Ltd	1904	Brill 27Cx	4 x 25hp	Cross bench open	56	35'0" 10.66m	6'3" 1.90m	10'6" 3.20m	Stored
30	ER&TCW Ltd	1904	Brill 27Cx	4 x 25hp	Cross bench open	56	35'0" 10.66m	6'3" 1.90m	10'6" 3.20m	Stored
31	ER&TCW Ltd	1904	Brill 27Cx	4 x 25hp	Cross bench open	56	35'0" 10.66m	6'3" 1.90m	10'6" 3.20m	Stored
32	UEC	1906	Brill 27Cx	4 x 27.5hp	Cross bench open	56	35'0" 10.66m	6'3" 1.90m	10'6" 3.20m	In service
33	UEC	1906	Brill 27Cx	4 x 27.5hp	Cross bench open	56	35'0" 10.66m	6'3" 1.90m	10'6" 3.20m	In service
34	IOMR	1995/6	Milnes Special	4x 25hp	Works Loco	Nil	27'8" 8.43m	6'7" 2.00m	10'0" 3.04m	In Service

MANX ELECTRIC RAILWAY TRAILER CARS (3'0" Gauge)

No.	Built by	Year	Bogies	Car Type	No. of seats	Length	Width	Height	Notes
13	Milnes	1893	Milnes S1	Cross bench open	44	28'9" 8.76m	6'3" 1.90m	9'2" 2.79m	In service
36	Milnes	1894	Milnes S2	Cross bench open	44	29'0" 8.83m	6'1" 1.85m	9'0" 2.74m	Stored
37	Milnes	1894	Milnes S2	Cross bench open	44	29'0" 8.83m	6'1" 1.85m	9'0" 2.74m	In service
40	English Electric	1930	Milnes S1	Cross bench open	44	28'8" 8.73m	6'5" 1.95m	9'7" 2.92m	In service
41	English Electric	1930	Milnes S1	Cross bench open	44	28'8" 8.73m	6'5" 1.95m	9'7" 2.92m	In service
42	Milnes	1903	Milnes S3	Cross bench open	44	28'6" 8.68m	6'5" 1.95m	9'5" 2.87m	In service
43	Milnes	1903	Milnes S3	Cross bench open	44	28'6" 8.68m	6'5" 1.95m	9'5" 2.87m	In service
44	English Electric	1930	Milnes S1	Cross bench open	44	28'8" 8.73m	6'5" 1.95m	9'7" 2.92m	In service
46	Milnes	1899	Milnes S1	Cross bench open	44	28'8" 8.73m	6'5" 1.95m	9'10" 3.0m	In service
47	Milnes	1899	Milnes S1	Cross bench open	44	28'8" 8.73m	6'5" 1.95m	9'10" 3.0m	In service
48	Milnes	1899	Milnes S2	Cross bench open	44	28'8" 8.73m	6'5" 1.95m	9'10" 3.0m	In service
49	Milnes	1893	Milnes S1	Cross bench open	44	28'9" 8.76m	6'3" 1.90m	9'2" 2.79m	In service
50	Milnes	1893	Milnes S1	Cross bench open	44	28'9" 8.76m	6'3" 1.90m	9'2" 2.79m	Stored
53	Milnes	1893	Milnes S1	Cross bench open	44	28'9" 8.76m	6'3" 1.90m	9'2" 2.79m	Stored
54	Milnes	1893	Milnes S1	Cross bench open	44	28'9" 8.76m	6'3" 1.90m	9'2" 2.79m	Stored
55	ER&TCC	1904	Brill 27CxT	Cross bench open	44	29'4" 8.94m	6'5" 1.95m	9'4" 2.84m	Stored
56	ER&TCC	1904/ 1995	Brill 27CxT	Disabled Access Trailer		29'4" 8.94m	6'5" 1.95m	9'4" 2.84m	In service
57	ER&TCC	1904	Brill 27CxT	Unvestibuled saloon	32	32'9" 9.98m	6'9" 2.05m	10'8" 3.25m	In service
58	ER&TCC	1904	Brill 27CxT	Unvestibuled saloon	32	32'9" 9.98m	6'9" 2.05m	10'8" 3.25m	In service
59	Milnes	1895	Milnes S2	Unvestibuled saloon	18	22'2" 6.75m	6'9" 2.05m	10'10" 3.30m	In service
60	Milnes	1896	Milnes S1	Cross bench open	44	28'9" 8.76m	5'9" 1.75m	8'7" 2.62m	In service
61	UEC	1906	Brill 27CxT	Cross bench open	44	29'4" 8.94m	6'5" 1.95m	9'4" 2.84m	In service
62	UEC	1906	Brill 27CxT	Cross bench open	44	29'4" 8.94m	6'5" 1.95m	9'4" 2.84m	In service

Trailer car numbering.

Trailers are listed here in current numerical order. Except for No. 13, these are the numbers they have carried since 1906 when the final power cars were delivered. Before 1906 many of the trailers were re-numbered, some several times when it was necessary to release numbers for new power cars. As an example of this, the first three trailers started life as 11-13, then became 23-25, then 28-30 and finally 49-51 (51 reverted to 13 for the centenary celebrations in 1993 and still carries this number).

MANX ELECTRIC RAILWAY FREIGHT STOCK (3'0" Gauge)

No.	Built by	Year	Bogies	Type	Length	Width	Height	Notes
1	Milnes	1894	—	6-ton 3-Plank Open	13'2" 4.01m	6'0" 1.82m	4'11" 1.50m	In service
3	Milnes	1894	—	6-ton van (with platform)	16'5" 5.01m	6'6" 1.98m	9'5" 2.88m	Stored Dhoon Quarry
4	Milnes	1894	—	6-ton van (with platforms)	16'5" 5.01m	6'6" 1.98m	9'5" 2.88m	In service Red Livery
7	Milnes	1897/8	—	6-ton -Plank Open	13'3" 4.04m	5'10" 1.77m	4'11" 1.5m	In service

No.	Built by	Year	Bogies	Type	Length	Width	Height	Notes
8	Milnes	1897/8	—	6-ton	13'3"	5'10"	4'11"	Withdrawn 1998
				-Plank Open	4.04m	1.77m	1.5m	.
10	Milnes	1897/8	—	6-ton	13'3"	5'10"	4'11"	Restoration
				-Plank Open	4.04m	1.77m	1.5m	in progress
11	Milnes	1898/9	—	6-ton van(with platforms)	12'7"	6'6"	9'10"	Jurby Transport
					3.83m	1.98m	3.0m	Museum
12	Milnes	1898/9	—	6-ton van(with platforms)	12'7"	6'6"	9'10"	Chassis only
					3.83m	1.98m	3.0m	Stored Dhoon Quarry
13	Milnes	1903/4	—	5-ton van	10'10"	5'10"	8'8"	Stored
					3.30m	1.77m	2.64m	Dhoon Quarry
14	Milnes	1903/4	—	5-ton van	10'10"	5'10"	8'8"	In service
					3.30m	1.77m	2.64m	
16	MER	1908	—	6-ton van	12'10"	6'8"	9'3"	Stored
					3.92m	2.04m	2.83m	Dhoon Quarry
21	MER	1926	Milnes	Engineers Flat	32'3"	6'5"	3'4"	In service
					9.84m	1.97m	1.01m	
26	Milnes/ MER	1895		Bogie freight trailer	35'7"	6'9"	10'0"	Stored
					10.85m	2.05m	3.04m	
45	Milnes	1899	Milnes S2	Engineers flat	28'8"	6'5"	9'10"	In service
					8.73m	1.95m	3.0m	
52	Milnes	1893	Milnes S1	Overhead Wiring Trailer	28'9"	6'3"		In service
					8.76m	1.90m		

SNAEFELL MOUNTAIN RAILWAY POWER CARS (3'6" Gauge)

No.	Built by	Year	Bogies	Motors	Car Type	No. of seats	Length	Width	Height	Notes
1	Milnes	1895	Milnes Special	4x 25hp	Vestibuled Saloon	46	35'7 " 10.85m	7'3" 2.20m	10'4" 3.16m	In service
2	Milnes	1895	Milnes Special	4x 25hp	Vestibuled Saloon	46	35'7 " 10.85m	7'3" 2.20m	10'4" 3.16m	In service
3	Milnes	1895	Milnes Special	4x 25hp	Vestibuled Saloon	46	35'7 " 10.85m	7'3" 2.20m	10'4" 3.16m	In service
4	Milnes	1895	Milnes Special	4x 25hp	Vestibuled Saloon	46	35'7 " 10.85m	7'3" 2.20m	10'4" 3.16m	In service
5	H Kinnan (Ramsey)	1971	Milnes Special	4x 25hp	Vestibuled Saloon	48	35'7 " 10.85m	7'3" 2.20m	10'4" 3.16m	In service
6	Milnes	1895	Milnes Special	4x 25hp	Vestibuled Saloon	46	35'7 " 10.85m	7'3" 2.20m	10'4" 3.16m	In service

Notes: As built these cars had unglazed windows; glazed sliding windows were fitted by April 1896
The lack of ventilation, when all windows were closed in sunny but windy weather, resulted in clerestory windows being fitted during the winter of 1896/97.
The seating capacity was increased to 48 by the addition of two single seats, one at each end backing onto the bulkhead.
Between 1977 and 1979, all six cars were fitted with new bogies built by London Transport at their Acton works and with 4 x 61hp traction motors and control equipment from seven tramcars Nos 1003/04/05/08/09/10/11 bought from Aachen in Germany.

SNAEFELL MOUNTAIN RAILWAY FREIGHT STOCK (3'6" Gauge)

No.	Built by	Year	Bogies	Type	Length	Width	Height	Notes
—	IOMR	1981/82	—	?-ton 3-Plank Open	11'9" 3.58m	5'1" 1.54m	4'5" 1.34m	On replaced power car bogie sides. Damaged in Runaway c1990 Rebuilt and In service
				Flat Wagon	7'6" 2.28m	4'9" 1.44m	1'10" 0.55m	Formerly at ? Purchased from Patrick Keefe In Service
—	IOMR	1998	—	Tower wagon	13'0" 3.98m	5'0" 1.52m	14'2" 4.31m	On chassis from 3-Way tipper In service
	Allens of Tipton	1940 -42		Flat Wagon	8'4" 2.54m	4'2" 1.27m	2'6" 0.76m	Formerly Lochaber Rly 13/24-1,2 or 3

CIVIL AVIATION AUTHORITY RAILCARS (3'6" Gauge)
(For use on the Snaefell Mountain Railway)

No.	Builder	Date	Builder No.	Length	Width	Height	Wheel Arrangement	Weight	Notes
	D. Wickham Ware, Herts	1951	5864	9'5" 2.87m	5'7" 1.70m	7'9" 2.36m	4-wheel	2t 10cwt	Preserved Stratfold Barn Railway
3	D. Wickham Ware, Herts	1977	10956	12'9" 3.88m	7'8" 2.35m	8'1" 2.47m	4-wheel	3t 0cwt	In service
4	Wickham Rail Suckley, Worcestershire	1991	11730	13'4" 4.06m	7'8" 2.35m	8'6" 2.47m	4-wheel	4t 0cwt	In service

STEAM RAILWAY LOCOMOTIVES (3'0" Gauge)
Steam Locomotives

No	Name	Builder	Date	Builder's No.	Type	Length over Beams	Width	Coupled Wheel Diameter	Cylinders	Weight	Notes
1	Sutherland	Beyer Peacock	1873	1253	2-4-0T	21'0" 6.40m	6'9" 2.06m	3'9" 1.14m	11"x18" 28x46cm	17t 12cwt	Stored Dismantled
3	Pender	Beyer Peacock	1873	1255	2-4-0T	21'0" 6.40m	6'9" 2.06m	3'9" 1.14m	11"x18" 28x46cm	17t 12cwt	Manchester Museum of Science & Industry
4	Loch	Beyer Peacock	1874	1416	2-4-0T	21'0" 6.40m	6'9" 2.06m	3'9" 1.14m	11"x18" 28x46cm	17t 12cwt	In service
5	Mona	Beyer Peacock	1874	1417	2-4-0T	21'0" 6.40m	6'9" 2.06m	3'9" 1.14m	11"x18" 28x46cm	17t 12cwt	Stored Douglas
6	Peveril	Beyer Peacock	1875	1524	2-4-0T	21'0" 6.40m	6'9" 2.06m	3'9" 1.14m	11"x18" 28x46cm	17t 12cwt	Port Erin Museum
8	Fenella	Beyer Peacock	1894	3610	2-4-0T	21'0" 6.40m	6'9" 2.06m	3'9" 1.14m	11"x18" 28x46cm	17t 12cwt	In service
9	Douglas	Beyer Peacock	1896	3815	2-4-0T	21'0" 6.40m	6'9" 2.06m	3'9" 1.14m	11"x18" 28x46cm	17t 12cwt	Stored Douglas
10	G H Wood	Beyer Peacock	1905	4662	2-4-0T	21'0" 6.40m	6'9" 2.06m	3'9" 1.14m	11"x18" 28x46cm	20t 10cwt	In service
11	Maitland	Beyer Peacock	1905	4663	2-4-0T	21'0" 6.40m	6'9" 2.06m	3'9" 1.14m	11"x18" 28x46cm	20t 10cwt	In service
12	Hutchinson	Beyer Peacock	1908	5126	2-4-0T	21'0" 6.40m	6'9" 2.06m	3'9" 1.14m	11"x18" 28x46cm	20t 10cwt	In service
13	Kissack	Beyer Peacock	1910	5382	2-4-0T	21'0" 6.40m	6'9" 2.06m	3'9" 1.14m	11"x18" 28x46cm	20t 10cwt	In service
14	Thornhill	Beyer Peacock	1880	2028	2-4-0T	21'0" 6.40m	6'9" 2.06m	3'9" 1.14m	11"x18" 28x46cm	17t 12cwt	Privately preserved on the Island
15	Caledonia	Dubs & Co.	1885	2178	0-6-0T	22'0" 6.71m	6'10" 2.08m	3'3" 0.99m	13"x20" 33x51cm	23t 11cwt	In service
16	Mannin	Beyer Peacock	1926	6296	2-4-0T	21'0" 6.40m	7'2" 2.18m	3'9" 1.14m	12"x18" 30x46cm	23t 9cwt	Port Erin Museum

Diesel Locomotives and Railcars

No.	Name	Builder	Date	Builder's No.	Length	Width	Height	Wheel Arrangement	Weight	Notes
17	Viking	Schoema	1958	2175	20'0" 6.10m	7'2" 2.20m	8'10" 2.70m	4-wheel	21t 0cwt	In service
18	Ailsa	Hunslet Engine Co.	1994	LD9342	20'5" 6.23m	5'7" 1.71m	8'2" 2.49m	4-Wheel	?	In service
19		Walker/ GNR(I)	1949	79789	41'3" 12.56m	7'6" 2.28m	9'11" 3.02m	Diesel Railcar		Stored Partially Rebuilt
20		Walker/ GNR(I)	1950	83149	41'3" 12.56m	7'6" 2.28m	9'11" 3.02m	Diesel Railcar		Stored Partially Rebuilt
		Motorail Ltd	1959	22021 /59	7'5" 2.26m	4'0" 1.21m	4'6" 1.37m	4-wheel	4t 20cwt	In service
		Motorail Ltd	1966	40s280	7'5" 2.26m	4'0" 1.21m	6'0" 1.82m	4-wheel	4t 20cwt	In service
		Wickham Ltd T27	1956	7442	8'0" 2.43m	5'7" 1.70m	6'10" 2.08m	4-wheel		In service
		Wickham Ltd T27a	1961	8849	8'0" 2.43m	5'7" 1.70m	6'10" 2.08m	4-wheel		In service

Jackson	153202	14'11" 4.55m	6'3" 1.90m	9'4" 2.84m	4-Wheel Tamping		In Service

STEAM RAILWAY PASSENGER COACHES (3'O" Gauge)

No.	Built by	Year	Coach Type	No. of Seats	Length	Width	Height	Notes
F6	Brown Marshalls	1876	Bogie Brake Composite	42	35'0" 10.66m	7'0" 2.13m	9'4" 2.84m	Sold to Mr Rampton Off Island
F9	Brown Marshalls	1881	Bogie Brake Composite	60	35'0" 10.66m	7'0" 2.13m	9'4" 2.84m	In service
F10	Brown Marshalls	1881	Bogie Brake Composite	60	35'0" 10.66m	7'0" 2.13m	9'4" 2.84m	In service
F11	Brown Marshalls	1881	Bogie Brake Composite	60	35'0" 10.66m	7'0" 2.13m	9'4" 2.84m	In service
F15	Brown Marshalls	1894	Bogie Brake Composite	42	35'0" 10.66m	7'0" 2.13m	9'4" 2.84m	Stored
F18	Brown Marshalls	1894	Bogie Brake Composite	50	35'0" 10.66m	7'0" 2.13m	9'4" 2.84m	In service
F21	MRCW Saltley	1896	Bogie Brake Composite	42	35'11" 10.94m	7'0" 2.13m	9'4" 2.84m	Sold to WHR, then to Ireland Returned to IOM 1998, now stored
F23	MRCW Saltley	1896	Bogie Brake Composite	42	35'11" 10.94m	7'0" 2.13m	9'4" 2.84m	Body broken up February 1983 Chassis to Weedkiller. In service
F25	MRCW Saltley	1896	Bogie Brake 3rd	60	35'0" 10.66m	7'0" 2.13m	9'4" 2.84m	Stored
F26	MRCW Saltley	1896	Bogie Brake 3rd	60	35'0" 10.66m	7'0" 2.13m	9'4" 2.84m	In service
F27	MRCW Saltley	1897	Bogie Luggage Van	—	35'0" 10.66m	7'0" 2.13m	9'4" 2.84m	Stored
F28	MRCW Saltley	1897	Bogie Luggage Van	—	35'0" 10.66m	7'0" 2.13m	9'4" 2.84m	Stored
F29	MRCW Saltley	1905	Bogie Vestibule Open 3rd	32	36'11" 11.25m	7'0" 2.13m	10'3" 3.12m	In service
F30	MRCW Saltley	1905	Bogie Vestibule Open 3rd	32	36'11" 11.25m	7'0" 2.13m	10'3" 3.12m	Dismantled awaiting rebuild
F31	MRCW Saltley	1905	Bogie Vestibule Open 3rd	32	36'11" 11.25m	7'0" 2.13m	10'3" 3.12m	In service
F32	MRCW Saltley	1905	Bogie Vestibule Open 3rd	32	36'11" 11.25m	7'0" 2.13m	10'3" 3.12m	Dismantled awaiting rebuild
F33	MRCW Saltley	1905	Bogie Guard Brake 3rd		37'0" 11.27m	7'0" 2.13m	10'0" 3.04m	Body broken up Chassis in use as a 'Runner'
F35	MRCW Saltley	1905	Bogie Vestibule Open 1st/3rd	41	36'11" 11.25m	7'0" 2.13m	10'3" 3.12m	In service
F36	MRCW Saltley	1905	Bogie Vestibule Open 1st/3rd	41	36'11" 11.25m	7'0" 2.13m	10'3" 3.12m	Port Erin Museum
F37	Hurst Nelson	1899	Bogie Guard Brake 1st/3rd		35'6" 10.82m	7'1" 2.32m	10'0" 3.04m	Sold to Mr Rampton Off Island
F38	Hurst Nelson	1899	Bogie Brake 3rd		35'6" 10.82m	7'1" 2.32m	10'0" 3.04m	Sold to Mr Rampton Off Island
F39	Bristol & South Wales RW Co	1887	Bogie Guard Brake 3rd		30'0" 9.14m	7'2" 2.18m	9'6" 2.89m	Used as Camping coach 1968-? In service
F40	MRCW Saltley	1907	Bogie Guard Brake 3rd		37'0" 11.27m	7'0" 2.13m	10'0" 3.04m	Body broken up Chassis in use as a 'Runner'
F43	MRCW Saltley	1908	Bogie Guard Brake 3rd		37'0" 11.27m	7'0" 2.13m	10'0" 3.04m	Stored
F44	MRCW Saltley	1908	Bogie Guard Brake 3rd		37'0" 11.27m	7'0" 2.13m	10'0" 3.04m	Body broken up 1983 Chassis in use as a 'Runner'
F45	MRCW Saltley	1913	Bogie Guard Brake 3rd		36'11" 11.25m	7'0" 2.13m	10'1" 3.07m	In service
F46	MRCW Saltley	1913	Bogie Guard Brake 3rd		36'11" 11.25m	7'0" 2.13m	10'1" 3.07m	In service
F47	MRCW Saltley	1923	Bogie Brake 3rd		36'11 11.25m	7'0" 2.13m	10'1" 3.07m	In service
F48	MRCW Saltley	1923	Bogie Brake 3rd		36'11" 11.25m	7'0" 2.13m	10'1" 3.07m	In service
F49	MRCW Saltley	1926	Bogie Guard Brake 3rd		37'0" 11.27m	7'0" 2.13m	10'0" 3.04m	In service
F50	MRCW Saltley (Frame) with Bodies B7 & B8	1925	Bogie 3rd	60	33'2" 10.10m	7'0" 2.13m	9'4" 2.84m	Body broken up 1974 Chassis in use as a 'Runner'

No.	Built by	Year	Type		Length	Width	Height	Notes
F54	MRCW Saltley (Frame) with Bodies A7 & C10	1923	Bogie Guard Composite	50	34'2" 10.41m	7'0" 2.13m	9'4" 2.84m	Body broken up New body 1997. In service
F57	MRCW Saltley (Frame) with Bodies B16 & B20	1919	Bogie 3rd	60	33'2" 10.10m	7'0" 2.13m	9'4" 2.84m	Body broken up December 1995 Chassis in use as a 'Runner'
F62	MRCW Saltley (Frame) with Bodies A1 & B1	1926	Bogie Composite	60	34'2" 10.41m	7'0" 2.13m	9'4" 2.84m	Stored
F63	MRCW Saltley (Frame) with Bodies B6 & B10	1920	Bogie 3rd	60	33'2" 10.10m	7'0" 2.13m	9'4" 2.84m	Stored
F64	MRCW Saltley (Frame) with Bodies B19 & C1	1912	Bogie 3rd	60	33'2" 10.10m	7'0" 2.13m	9'4" 2.84m	Body part burnt at Port Erin 1978 Half of body (C1) currently stored Chassis exchanged with F66 1979. Fitted with 'M' wagon sides. In service
F65	MRCW Saltley (Frame) with Bodies B22 & C7	1910	Bogie 3rd	60	33'2" 10.10m	7'0" 2.13m	9'4" 2.84m	Body broken up 1973 Chassis to Runner
F66	MRCW Saltley (Frame) with Bodies B11 & B15	1920	Bogie 3rd	60	33'2" 10.10m	7'0" 2.13m	9'4" 2.84m	Chassis exchanged with F64 and body rebuilt 1979. Stored Port St Mary
F67	MRCW Saltley (Frame) with Bodies B23 & C14	1922	Bogie3rd	60	33'2" 10.10m	7'0" 2.13m	9'4" 2.84m	Stored Port St Mary
F68	MRCW Saltley Frame) with Bodies A9 & C13	1909	Bogie Composite	60	34'2" 10.41m	7'0" 2.13m	9'4" 2.84m	Sold to Mr Rampton Off Island
F70	MRCW Saltley (Frame) with Bodies B9 & B14	1922	Bogie 3rd	60	33'2" 10.10m	7'0" 2.13m	9'4" 2.84m	Body broken up Chassis to twin Ballast Hopper
F71	MRCW Saltley (Frame) with Bodies B12 & C5	1911	Bogie 3rd	60	33'2" 10.10m	7'0" 2.13m	9'4" 2.84m	Body broken up Chassis in use as a 'Runner'
F73	MRCW Saltley (Frame) with Bodies A4 & D1	1920	Bogie Composite	60	34'2" 10.41m	7'0" 2.13m	9'4" 2.84m	Body broken up Chassis in use as a 'Runner'
F74	MRCW Saltley (Frame) with Bodies A11 & C11	1921	Bogie Composite	60	34'2" 10.41m	7'0" 2.13m	9'4" 2.84m	Stored Port St Mary
F75	MRCW Saltley (Frame) with Bodies A12 & C9	1926	Bogie Saloon		34'2" 10.41m	7'0" 2.13m	9'4" 2.84m	Port Erin Museum
N40	Swansea Wagon Company	1879	6w 1st	42	30'0" 9.14m	6'9" 2.05m	9'6" 2.89m	Formerly MNR No 1, then IMR F40 Sold to Mr Rampton Off Island
N41	Swansea Wagon Company	1879	6w 1st	42	30'0" 9.14m	6'9" 2.05m	9'6" 2.89m	Formerly MNR No 2, then IMR F41 Body became mess hut at Douglas shed in1964. Chassis Scrap Manx Metals, Ballasalla 1974/75. Body now Stored
N42	Swansea Wagon Company	1879	6w Composite	60	30'0" 9.14m	6'9" 2.05m	9'6" 2.89m	Formerly MNR No 3, then IMR F42 Stored, Property of IOMR&TPS
N45	Swansea Wagon Company	1879	6w 3rd Guard	60	30'0" 9.14m	6'9" 2.05m	9'6" 2.89m	Formerly MNR No 6, then IMR F45 Privately preserved on the IOM
N51	Swansea Wagon Company	1879	6w 3rd	60	30'0" 9.14m	6'9" 2.05m	9'6" 2.89m	Formerly MNR No 14, then IMR F51 Sold to Mr Rampton Off Island

STEAM RAILWAY FREIGHT STOCK (3'0" Gauge)

No.	Built by	Year	Type	Length	Width	Height	Notes
G1	MRCW Saltley	1873	4w Van	14'6" 4.41m	6'6" 1.98m	8'11" 2.71m	Stored
G12	Swansea Wagon Co	1879	4w Van	15'3" 4.64m	6'6" 1.98m	7'7" 2.31m	Formerly MNR No 15 In service
G19	Isle of Man Railway Co	1921	4w Van	16'0" 4.87m	6'6" 1.98m	7'9" 2.36m	On chassis of E3 Stored
H1	MRCW Saltley	1873	6-ton 3-Plank Open	14'6" 4.41m	6'6" 1.98m	5'3" 1.60m	In Service Fully restored by the IOMSRSA
M69	MRCW Saltley	1926	6-ton 2-Plank Open	14'6" 4.41m	6'6" 1.98m	4'9" 1.44m	Remains stored

M70	MRCW Saltley	1926	6-ton	14'6"	6'6"	4'9"		Stored
			2-Plank Open	4.41m	1.98m	1.44m		
M78	MRCW Saltley	1926	6-ton	14'6"	6'6"	4'9"		Fully restored by the IOMSRSA 1997/98
			2-Plank Open	4.41m	1.98m	1.44m		In service
(2)	Richard C. Gibbins	1893	8-ton Hand Crane	17'2" 5.23m	6'2" 1.87m	16'6" 5.03m		In use until 1980s. Now on display at Union Mills Station site.
	IOMR	1998	Well Wagon	21'0" 6.40m	6'5" 1.96m	2'8" 0.81m		In service
	W G Bagnall	1929	Flat Wagon	10'1" 3.07m	5'6" 1.67m	2'6" 0.76m		Formerly Lochaber Railway 13/12-5 In service
	W G Bagnall	1929	Flat Wagon	10'1" 3.07m	5'6" 1.67m	2'6" 0.76m		Formerly Lochaber Railway 13/12-? In service
	W G Bagnall	1929	Flat Wagon	10'1" 3.07m	5'6" 1.67m	2'6" 0.76m		Formerly Lochaber Railway 13/12-? In service
	Allens of Tipton	1940 -42	2.5-ton Side Tipper	8'5" 2.56m	4'2" 1.27m	6'3" 1.90m		Formerly Lochaber Railway 13/24-5 In service
	Allens of Tipton	1940 -42	2.5-ton Side Tipper	8'5" 2.56m	4'2" 1.27m	6'3" 1.90m		Formerly Lochaber Railway 13/24-1,2 or 3 In service
	Allens of Tipton	1940 -42	2.5-ton Side Tipper	8'5" 2.56m	4'2" 1.27m	6'3" 1.90m		Formerly Lochaber Railway 13/24-1,2 or 3 In service
	Allens of Tipton (Chassis)	1940 -42	Passenger Vehicle	8'7" 2.61m	5'2" 1.57m	5'11" 1.80m		Formerly Lochaber Railway 13/24-6 In service
	Allens of Tipton (Chassis)	1940 -42	2.5-ton 5-Plank Open	8'5" 2.56m	5'7" 1.70m	4'8" 1.42m		Formerly Lochaber Railway 13/24-4 In service
			Flat Wagon	7'5" 2.26m	5'1" 1.54m	3'10" 1.16m		Formerly on Ramsey Pier Preserved Peel Transport Museum
			Boiler Movement	19'8" 5.99m	5'0" 1.53m	5'2" 1.58m		In service
			Ballast Hopper	19'8" 5.99m	5'0" 1.53m	7'4" 2.24m		In service

Note: Although these wagons are listed as on the Steam Railway, they sometimes are transferred to the Manx Electric if required. It is therefore possible that any or all of these wagons listed here, might be seen anywhere on the Island.

DOUGLAS HORSE TRAMWAY CARS (3'0" Gauge)

No.	Built by	Year	Car Type	No. of seats	Length	Floor Width	Overall Width	Height	Notes
1	Milnes Voss & Co	1913	S/D Saloon	30	24'8" 7.51m	6'4" 1.94m	6'7" 2.0m	9'11" 3.02m	In service
11	Starbuck C&W Co	1886	Toastrack	32	22'9" 6.93m	5'4" 1.62m	6'8" 2.03m	9'6" 2.89m	Stored Jurby
12	Milnes	1888	Toastrack	32	22'9" 6.93m	5'4" 1.62m	6'8" 2.03m	9'6" 2.89m	In service
14	MRCW Saltley	1883	Double Deck	42	22'6" 6.85m		6'0" 1.82m	10'8" 3.25m	Displayed Manx Museum Douglas
18	MRCW Saltley	1883	Double Deck	42	23'1" 7.03m	6'1" 1.85m	6'4" 1.93m	10'8" 3.25m	In service
21	Milnes	1890	Toastrack	40	24'8" 7.51m	5'4" 1.62m	6'11" 2.09m		In service
22	Milnes	1890	Toastrack	32	22'5" 6.83m	5'5" 1.65m	6'10" 2.08m	9'9" 2.79m	Converted to shop Stored
27	Milnes	1892	Winter saloon	30	24'5" 7.44m	5'10" 1.77m	6'6" 1.98m	9'2" 2.79m	In service
28	Milnes	1892	Winter saloon	30	24'5" 7.44m	5'10" 1.77m	6'6" 1.98m	9'2" 2.79m	In service
29	Milnes	1892	Winter saloon	30	24'5" 7.44m	5'10" 1.77m	6'6" 1.98m	9'2" 2.79m	In service
32	Milnes	1896	Toastrack	32	21'8" 6.60m	5'4" 1.62m	6'10" 2.08m	8'7" 2.61m	In service
33	Milnes	1896	Toastrack	32	21'8" 6.60m	5'4" 1.62m	6'10" 2.08m	8'7" 2.61m	In service
34	Milnes	1896	Toastrack	32	21'8" 6.60m	5'4" 1.62m	6'10" 2.08m	8'7" 2.61m	In service
35	Milnes	1896	Toastrack	32	21'8" 6.60m	5'4" 1.62m	6'10" 2.08m	8'7" 2.61m	In service
36	Milnes	1896	Toastrack	40	24'11" 7.59m	5'4" 1.62m	6'10" 2.08m	8'7" 2.61m	In service
37	Milnes	1896	Toastrack	32	21'8" 6.60m	5'4" 1.62m	6'10" 2.08m	8'7" 2.61m	In service
38	Milnes	1902	Toastrack	40	24'5" 7.44m	5'5" 1.65m	6'11" 2.10m	8'7" 2.61m	In service

39	Milnes	1902	Toastrack	40	23'0" 7.01m	5'5" 1.65m	6'11" 2.10m	8'9" 2.67m	In service
40	Milnes	1902	Toastrack	40	24'5" 7.44m	5'4" 1.62m	6'10" 2.08m	8'11" 2.72m	In service
42	Milnes Voss & Co	1905	Toastrack	40	24'8" 7.51m	5'5" 1.65m	7'0" 2.13m	9'1" 2.77m	In service
43	United Electric Car Company	1907	Toastrack	40	24'6" 7.46m	5'5" 1.65m	6'11" 2.10m	8'10" 2.69m	In service
44	United Electric Car Company	1907	Toastrack	40	24'6" 7.46m	5'5" 1.65m	6'11" 2.10m	8'10" 2.69m	In service
45	Milnes Voss & Co	1908	Toastrack	40	25'0" 7.62m	5'6" 1.67m	7'0" 2.13m	8'6" 2.59m	In service
47	Milnes Voss & Co	1911	Toastrack	40	25'1" 7.64m	5'5" 1.65m	7'0" 2.13m	8'9" 2.66m	Stored Jurby
49	Vulcan Motor	1935	Saloon/Toastrack Convertible	27/34	25'6" 7.77m	5'7" 1.70m	6'11" 2.10m	8'6" 2.59m	Stored Jurby

UPPER DOUGLAS CABLE TRAMWAY CARS (3'0" Gauge)

Car No.	Built by	Year	Bogies	Car Type	No. of seats	Length	Width	Height	Notes
72/73	Milnes	1896	Milnes	Cross bench	38	30'0" 9.14m	5'7" 1.70m	9'0" 2.74m	Preserved Jurby Transport Museum

DOUGLAS HEAD AND MARINE DRIVE TRAMWAY CARS (4'81/2" Gauge)

Car No.	Built by	Year	Chassis	Motors	Car Type	No. of seats	Length	Width	Height	Notes
1	Brush	1896	Lord Baltimore No 2	Westinghouse 2x25hp	Double Deck	75	29'5" 8.96m	7'4" 2.23m	14'4" 4.36m	Preserved Crich

GROUDLE GLEN RAILWAY LOCOMOTIVES (2'0" Gauge)
Steam Locomotives

Name	Builder	Date	Builder No	Type	Length over Beams	Width	Coupled Wheel Diameter	Cylinders	Weight	Notes
Sea Lion	W G Bagnall	1896	1484	2-4-0T	10'9" 3.28m	4'2" 1.27m	1'2" 0.36m	4"x7"	4t 12cwt	In service
Polar Bear	W G Bagnall	1905	1781	2-4-0T	11'0" 3.35m	4'2" 1.27m	1'3" 0.38m	5"x7"	5t 10cwt	Preserved Amberley Chalk Pits Museum
Annie	Richard Booth Isle of Man	1998		0-4-2T	10'10" 3.30m	4'2" 1.27m	1'4" 0.41m	5"x7"	4t 0cwt	In service

Electric Locomotives

No.	Name	Builder	Date	Builder's No.	Length	Width	Height	Wheel Arrangement	Weight	Notes
	Polar Bear	Alan Keefe	2006	313	9'7" 2.93m	4'2" 1.27m	6'4" 1.94m	4-wheel	4t 0cwt	In service

Diesel Locomotives

No.	Name	Builder	Date	Builder's No.	Length	Width	Height	Wheel Arrangement	Weight	Notes
1	Dolphin	Hunslet Engine Co.	1952	4394	8'11" 2.72m	3'5" 1.04m	5'0" 1.52m	4-wheel	5t 0cwt	In service
2	Walrus	Hunslet Engine Co.	1952	4395	8'11" 2.72m	3'5" 1.04m	5'0" 1.52m	4-wheel	5t 0cwt	In service
	Parracombe	E. E. Baguley Ltd	1947	3232	10'7" 3.22m	3'6" 1.07m	6'1" 1.85m	4-wheel		Restoration in Progress

GROUDLE GLEN RAILWAY PASSENGER COACHES (2'0" Gauge)

Coach No.	Built by	Year	Coach Type	No. of Seats	Length	Width	Height	Notes
1	G F Milnes	1896	4w Toastrack Type A	10	13'0" 3.96m	3'2" 0.96m	6'9" 2.06m	[1]
2	G F Milnes	1896	4w Toastrack Type A	10	13'0" 3.96m	3'2" 0.96m	6'9" 2.06m	[1]
3	G F Milnes	1896	4w Toastrack Type A	10	13'0" 3.96m	3'2" 0.96m	6'9" 2.06m	[1]
4	G F Milnes	1896	4w Toastrack Type B	10	13'0" 3.96m	3'2" 0.96m	6'9" 2.06m	[1]
5	G C Milnes Voss	1905	4w Toastrack Type C/D	10	13'0" 3.96m	3'2" 0.96m	6'9" 2.06m	[1]
6	G C Milnes Voss	1905	4w Toastrack Type C/D	10	13'0" 3.96m	3'2" 0.96m	6'9" 2.06m	[1]
7	G C Milnes Voss	1905	4w Toastrack Type C/D	10	13'0" 3.96m	3'2" 0.96m	6'9" 2.06m	[1]
8	G C Milnes Voss	1905	4w Toastrack Type C/D	10	13'0" 3.96m	3'2" 0.96m	6'9" 2.06m	[1]
1	GGR (J Bray)	1984	Bogie open	24	18'0" 5.49m	4'0" 1.22m	6'11" 2.11m	On former Doddington chassis and bogies In service
2	GGR (J Bray/ H Flavell)	1985	Bogie open	24	18'0" 5.49m	4'0" 1.22m	6'11" 2.11m	On former Doddington chassis and bogies In service
3	GGR (H Flavell)	1993	Bogie open	24	18'0" 5.49m	4'0" 1.22m	6'11" 2.11m	On former Doddington bogies, chassis built in Ramsey for GGR. In service

Note:

[1] Over the years, renumbering of these vehicles has taken place to the extent that individual identification is no longer possible. During the closure of the railway from 1962 to 1986, parts at least of the vehicles were dispersed to various locations, from which some have returned. The current position is:

3 vehicles (one each of types A, C and D) in service on the GGR, rebuilds/replicas.
Various parts on the GGR from which a further rebuild/replica is under construction.
2 vehicles (one each of types A and D) in service at the Amberley Chalk Pits Museum, rebuilds/replicas, plus one c1990 built complete replica, type A.
1 vehicle derelict at Cadeby Light Railway, Leicestershire.

GROUDLE GLEN RAILWAY FREIGHT STOCK (2'0" Gauge)

No.	Built by	Year	Type	Length	Width	Height	Notes
1	Hudson, Leeds		2-Plank open Bomb wagon	9'0" 2.74m	5'4" 1.63m	3'8" 1.12m	Formerly MOD No. 73. In service
2	Hudson, Leeds		2-Plank open Bomb wagon	9'0" 2.74m	4'11" 1.50m	4'9" 1.45m	Formerly MOD No. 164. In service Sides and one end removed
3	Hudson, Leeds		2-Plank open Bomb wagon	8'9" 2.67m	5'4" 1.63m	3'5" 1.04m	Formerly MOD No. 92. In service Sides removed, now carries small tool chest.
4	Hudson, Leeds		2-Plank open Bomb wagon	8'1" 2.46m	5'4" 1.63m	3'7" 1.09m	Formerly MOD No. 179 or 183. In service Withdrawn. Derelict on site
5	Hudson, Leeds		2-Plank open Bomb wagon	8'10" 2.69m	5'4" 1.63m	3'8" 1.12m	Formerly MOD No. 179 or 183. In service Withdrawn. Derelict on site
	Hudson, Leeds		2-Plank open Bomb wagon	8'2" 2.49m	5'4" 1.63m		Formerly MOD No. 119 Withdrawn. Derelict on site
—	Hudson, Leeds		2-Plank open Bomb wagon	9'1" 2.77m	5'4" 1.63m	3'5" 1.04m	Formerly MOD No. 141 Withdrawn. Derelict on site
6	Allens, Tipton		Side tipper	5'5" 1.65m	2'7" 0.79m	4'0" 1.22m	In service
—			Side tipper	6'1" 1.85m	4'11" 1.50m	3'11" 1.19m	On display at Groudle
—	GGR		Bogie open	18'6" 5.65m	3'6" 1.08m	2'0" 0.63m	In service
—	Hudson, Leeds		Brake Van	8'9" 2.68m	3'11" 1.19m	7'4" 2.24m	In service

GREAT LAXEY MINES RAILWAY LOCOMOTIVES (1'7" Gauge)

Steam Locomotives

Name	Builder	Date	Builder No	Type	Length over Beams	Width	Coupled Wheel Diameter	Cylinders	Weight	Notes
Ant	Gt Northern Steam	2004	(684)	0-4-0T	8'7" 2.62m	3'0" 0.92m	2'0" 0.60m	4"x6"	2t 0cwt	In service
Bee	Gt Northern Steam	2004	(685)	0-4-0T	8'7" 2.62m	3'0" 0.92m	2'0" 0.60m	4"x6"	2t 0cwt	In service

Electric Locomotives

No.	Name	Builder	Date	Builder's No.	Length	Width	Height	Wheel Arrangement	Weight	Notes
	Wasp	Clayton	1973	B0152	7'2" 2.19m	2'3" 0.67m	3'7" 1.09m	4-Wheel		In Service

GREAT LAXEY MINES RAILWAY PASSENGER COACHES (1'7" Gauge)

No.	Built by	Year	Type	Length	Width	Height	Notes
1	Alan Keefe		Bogie Tunnel	12'11" 3.95m	3'8" 1.11m	5'4" 1.62m	In service
2	Alan Keefe		Bogie Tunnel	13'1" 3.99m	3'8" 1.11m	5'1" 1.54m	In service

GREAT LAXEY MINES RAILWAY FREIGHT STOCK (1'7" Gauge)

No.	Built by	Year	Type	Length	Width	Height	Notes
	Laxey Blacksmith	2000	4w-Tipper	5'11" 1.80m	1'10" 0.55m	3'3" 1.00m	In service
	Laxey Blacksmith	2000	4w-Tipper	5'11" 1.80m	1'10" 0.55m	3'3" 1.00m	In service
	Laxey Blacksmith	2000	4w-Tipper	5'11" 1.80m	1'10" 0.55m	3'3" 1.00m	In service
	Laxey Blacksmith	2000	4w-Tipper	5'11" 1.80m	1'10" 0.55m	3'3" 1.00m	In service
	Laxey Blacksmith	2000	4w-Tipper	5'11" 1.80m	1'10" 0.55m	3'3" 1.00m	In service
	Laxey Blacksmith	2000	4w-Tipper	5'11" 1.80m	1'10" 0.55m	3'3" 1.00m	In service
	Laxey Mines Railway	1999	4w-Flat	5'0" 1.52m	2'0" 0.60m	1'6" 0.46m	In Service Nicknamed Jimmy

Bibliography

Isle of Man Tramways, F K Pearson, David & Charles 1970, ISBN 0 7153 4740 3

Cliff Railways of the British Isles, Keith Turner, Oakwood Press 2002, ISBN 0 85361 594 2

Pier Railways and Tramways of the British Isles, Keith Turner, Oakwood Press 1999, ISBN 0 85361 541 1

Railways and Tramways of the Isle of Man, Barry Edwards, OPC 1993, ISBN 0 86093 507 8

Isle of Man Steam Railway, Barry Edwards, B&C Publications 1996, ISBN 0 9527756 0 3

The Manx Electric Railway, Barry Edwards, B&C Publications 1998, ISBN 0 9527756 2 X

Isle of Man Railways Locomotive, Tram and Rolling Stock Directory, Barry Edwards,
B&C Publications 1996, ISBN 0 9527756 3 8

Snaefell Mountain Railway 1895-1995, Barry Edwards, Midland Publishing 1995, ISBN 0 85780 031 1

The Douglas Horse Tramway, Keith Pearson, Adam Gordon 1999, ISBN 1 874422 25 7

Trams of the Isle of Man, Stan Basnett, Lily Publications 2009, ISBN 978 1 899602 19 3

Trains of the Isle of Man; The Twilight Years, Stan Basnett, Lily Publications 2008, ISBN 978 1 899602 23 0

Trains of the Isle of Man; The Ailsa Years, Stan Basnett, Lily Publications 2008, ISBN 978 1 899602 63 6

Trains of the Isle of Man; Post Nationalisation, Stan Basnett, Lily Publications 2008, ISBN 978 1 899602 04 9

The Isle of Man Railway Volume 1, J I C Boyd, Oakwood Press 1993, ISBN 0 85361 444 X

The Isle of Man Railway Volume 2, J I C Boyd, Oakwood Press 1994, ISBN 0 85361 469 5

The Isle of Man Railway Volume 3, J I C Boyd, Oakwood Press 1996, ISBN 0 85361 479 2

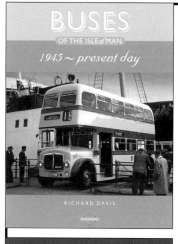

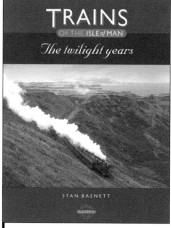

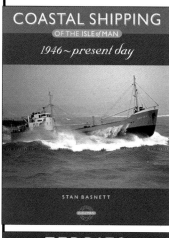

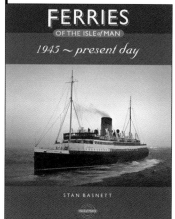